MEL BAY PRESENTS

MANDOLIN SAMPLER
BY DAN GELO

CD CONTENTS

#	Track	Page
1	The Carraroe/Frainc a' Phoill's Jigs [2:33]	6
2	Pizzicato Rag [1:12]	12
3	Agrigento [2:03]	18
4	Uncle Dave Medley [2:06]	23
5	Homage to Fauré [2:16]	29
6	Southern Railroad Locomotive Blues [0:57]	35
7	Maverick Creek [1:19]	40
8	Angel Dance [1:47]	44
9	Raritan Ride [1:18]	47
10	Miller's Reel [1:25]	52
11	Double-Talkin' Blues [1:44]	57
12	Big Sciota [1:50]	61
13	Jethritis [1:53]	67
14	Father's Day [1:54]	72

Recording Engineer: Mark Rubinstein

Mandolin on the left courtesy of Michael Kelly™ Guitar Company, www.michaelkellyguitars.com

1 2 3 4 5 6 7 8 9 0

© 2004 BY MEL BAY PUBLICATIONS, INC., PACIFIC, MO 63069.
ALL RIGHTS RESERVED. INTERNATIONAL COPYRIGHT SECURED. B.M.I. MADE AND PRINTED IN U.S.A.
No part of this publication may be reproduced in whole or in part, or stored in a retrieval system, or transmitted in any form
or by any means, electronic, mechanical, photocopy, recording, or otherwise, without written permission of the publisher.

Visit us on the Web at www.melbay.com — E-mail us at email@melbay.com

Contents

About the Author..3

Introduction...4

The Carraroe/Frainc a' Phoill's Jigs..6

Pizzicato Rag...12

Agrigento...18

Uncle Dave Medley...23

Homage to Fauré...29

Southern Railroad Locomotive Blues...35

Maverick Creek...40

Angel Dance..44

Raritan Ride...47

Miller's Reel..52

Double-Talkin' Blues..57

Big Sciota..61

Jethritis..67

Father's Day..72

About the Author

Dan Gelo was born and raised in northern New Jersey. Dan began studying guitar at age eight and later added mandolin, banjo, and fiddle to his roster of instruments. His teachers included the multi-instrumentalist and composer Eugene Ettore, chord solo stylist John Pariso, and Gene Lowinger, the concert violinist who toured as a member of Bill Monroe's Blue Grass Boys. He developed a passion for roots music of all kinds, from traditional Irish music to bluegrass to rockabilly, and earned a living teaching music and playing in a variety of bands and studios around New York. Dan's admiration for the great folk song collectors such as John and Alan Lomax led him to the formal study of anthropology, and he earned advanced degrees from Rutgers University.

Today Dan is an anthropology professor at the University of Texas in San Antonio. His scholarly publications include articles and books on the music and folk traditions of the Comanche Indians, and three award-winning film documentaries on the Indians of Texas. When he is not lecturing or conducting field work with Native Americans, Dan continues to compose and perform on mandolin and acoustic guitar. Dan's two books, *Fiddle Tunes and Irish Music for Mandolin* and *Fiddle Tunes and Irish Music for Guitar* were among the first in the Mel Bay catalog to feature Celtic stylings.

Introduction

The mandolin is today arguably more popular, and more frequently heard, than at any time since the era of the great mandolin orchestras in the 1910s. Like a lot of players who started on guitar (after seeing the Beatles on *The Ed Sullivan Show*) and who picked up the mandolin during the early 1970s bluegrass revival, I have marveled at the ever-expanding repertoire available to modern players. Equally exciting has been the appearance more and more of mandolin in popular and commercial music, to the point that every day you can hear its beautiful texture on the radio and TV. Add to this the increased availability of outstanding hand crafted instruments of various design, and there can be no doubt that we are living in a mandolin golden age.

Regardless of their instrument or the style for which they are renowned, many of the best musicians emphasize the importance of challenging themselves with music from different genres. A great variety of music has always been accessible to mandolinists, since the instrument readily bridges the folk and art realms. In recent years, however, more mandolin players seem receptive to the treasures that can be found over the near musical horizon — they seem more willing to range across (or disregard, or purposefully blur) stylistic boundaries. In a sense, contemporary players are rediscovering what the mandolin orchestra players knew long ago about the capacity of the instrument to carry us across a wide sonic and emotional territory, and we are having fun with this realization.

With the benefits of variety in mind I have developed this sampler of American mandolin music. Such a category as "American" mandolin must embrace examples rooted in Anglo-American folk tradition, including bluegrass and old-time country dance music; European folk styles; and blues, ragtime, and swing, with their direct African-American influences. There is also a genre that I refer to, for lack of a better term, as neoclassical--music that poses the mandolin as a modern art music instrument. You can no doubt think of still other kinds of "American" music that overlap with these or that might deserve separate recognition. My sampler is just that; not a complete inventory, but a selection. I hope these examples encourage you to explore yet other styles.

As a teaching tool, this collection has some direct aims. Overall, it is meant to help players move from the intermediate to the advanced level. What makes the tunes in this collection relatively advanced is that they tend to make several technical demands in a short space. Some of the more challenging techniques that are emphasized include:

> Cross-picking - Set right-hand picking patterns are played over shifting chord shapes, often to create arpeggios combining open and fretted strings.
>
> Rhythmic complexity for the right hand. Besides cross-picking patterns, in some places you'll find fast alternating picking, or patterns that imitate fiddle bow shuffles.
>
> Double stops - Sounding two courses at once fills out the sound and creates harmony; here there are some dissonant double-stops in the blues numbers and also fast tremoloed double stops as characteristic of early bluegrass.
>
> Pull-offs - Plucking the string with the left hand fingers is not that unusual for mandolin players; here the pull-offs are sometimes multiple and rapid-fire.

Drones - I've been interested in ways of making the mandolin more self-sufficient, so quite a few of the tunes use ringing open notes against which the melody moves. In some places these are higher strings and the effect is like that of the drone strings on a mountain dulcimer or five-string banjo. Elsewhere open "bass" notes are used insistently to ground the melody and imply chordal structure. In either case the mandolin has a fuller sound and so some of the arrangements can stand up as solos.

Voice leading in chord-melody - I think that the chord-melody potential of the mandolin has been underestimated and you will see in a few of the compositions here an effort to construct chord-melodies with unorthodox chord shapes.

Sheer speed - Speedy playing is overemphasized and overdone, but it is nice to be able to play fast when you want to!

The good news is that progress to the advanced playing level is largely a matter of working on these techniques slowly and in isolation. By spending time first working on sections of the songs, concentrating on the trickier passages by themselves, you will find that the entire songs are easier to learn, plus you will increase the array of techniques that you can transfer among tunes. Along the way I will highlight many of the techniques and musical ideas that can be practiced separately. A final aim of this collection is to give some insight into how new mandolin material can be composed. All of the tunes are either totally original or adaptations of traditional folk tunes in the public domain. In either case, the arrangements draw on a standard vocabulary of mandolin ideas and I try to use these in novel ways. If you develop an ear for such ideas and think about how they can be modified and recombined, you will be well on the way to creating mandolin music that will be fresh yet familiar, and uniquely your own. There is no better way to insure that the mandolin golden age will continue.

The Carraroe/Frainc a'Phoill's Jigs

These Irish jigs make a fine combination, especially since it is customary in Irish playing to string together two or more tunes. As far as I know, *The Carraroe* was first recorded by the Ballinakill Traditional Dance Players in 1931 and takes its name from the house of one of the band members, in County Galway. The second tune is from Donegal in the north of Ireland and it also goes by the name *King of the Pipers* (a title that in turn is also applied to at least one other tune). Under that name an arrangement appears in my book *Fiddle Tunes and Irish Music for Guitar.** The version here is different from my prior one and it owes a lot to the playing of fiddler Paddy Glackin.

The Carraroe is pretty straightforward. Measure 7 shows an optional double stop that can be added to change the melody slightly in the second pass. When joining a tune like this to another it is effective to have the guitar accompaniment vary, for example, dropping into only drones as the second tune kicks in to further emphasize the change. *Frainc a'Phoill's* is particularly interesting because it contains four rather than the usual two parts. In measures 70, 84, and 89-94 we see some ways of changing the melody as the group of four parts is repeated for a second time. Over the whole medley I attempt to get a kind of swinging rhythm going that is reminiscent of the wheezy phrasing of uillean pipes.

*Mel Bay Publications, 1985.

The Carraroe/Frainc a'Phoill's Jigs

Traditional
Arr. Dan Gelo

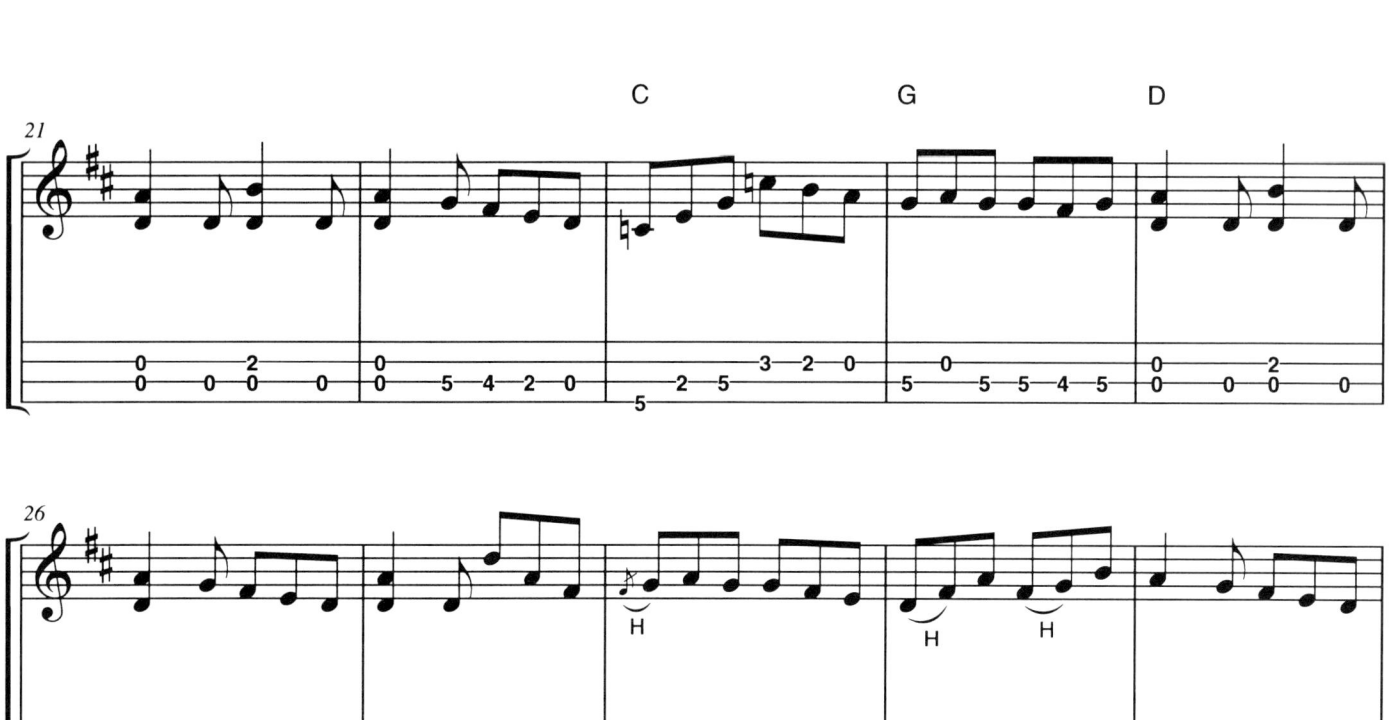
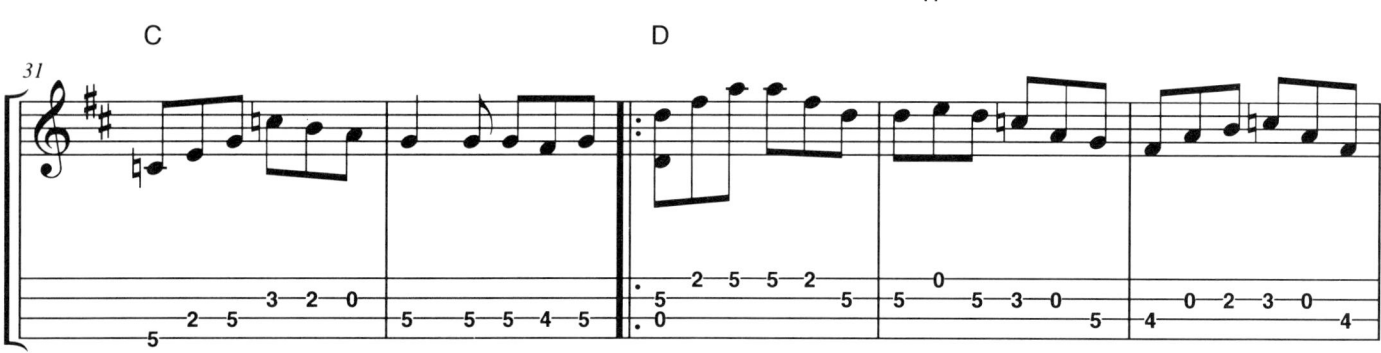

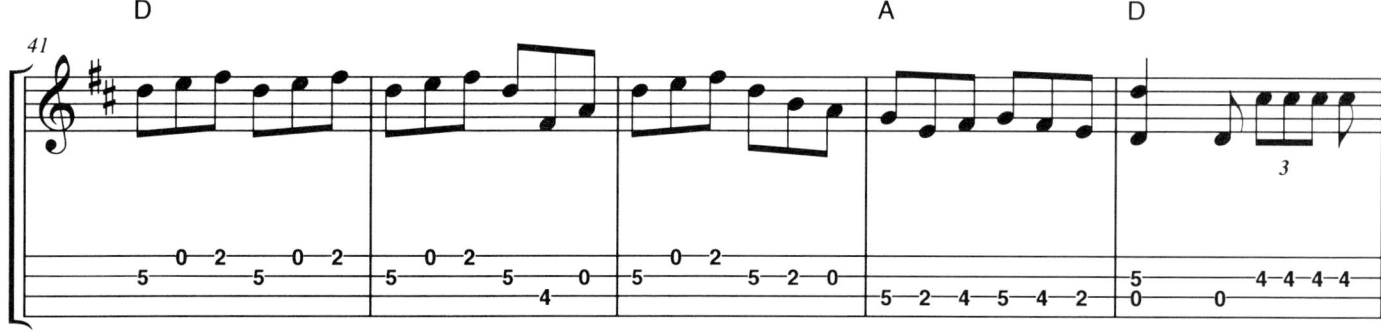

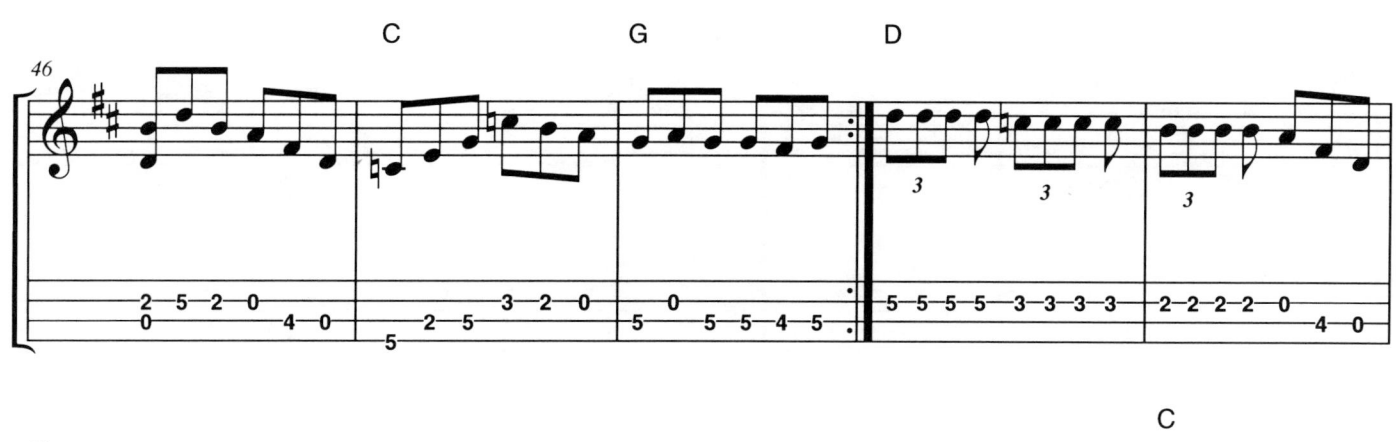
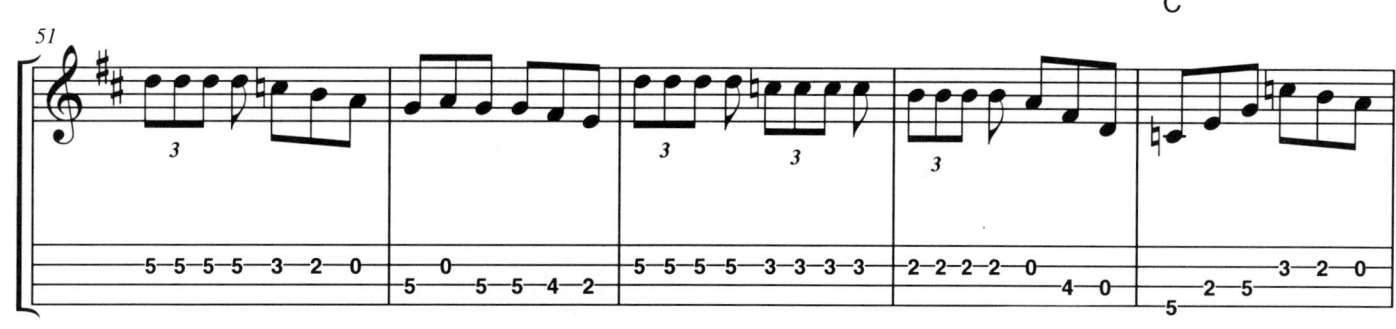
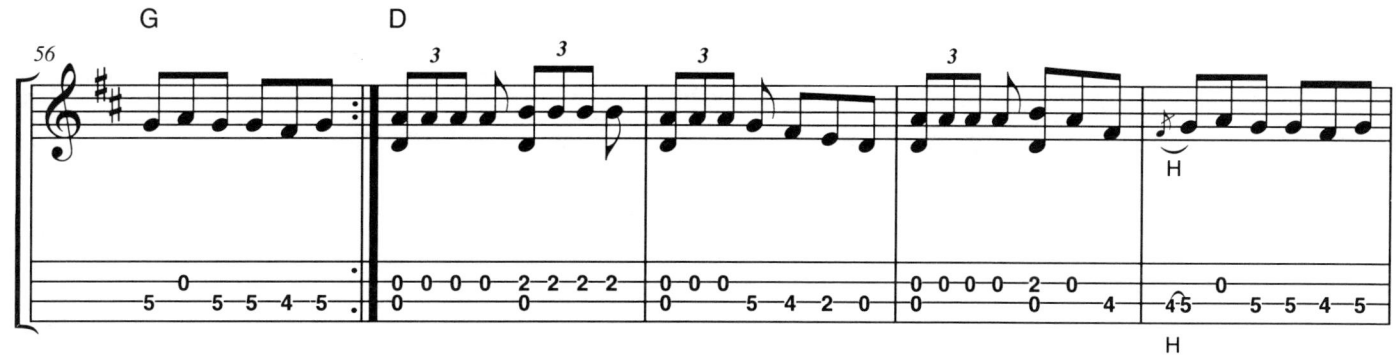
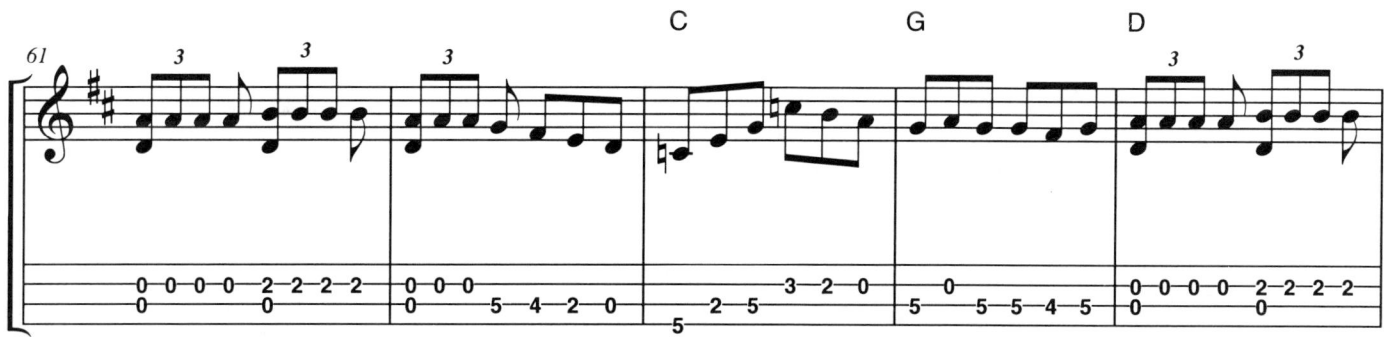

9

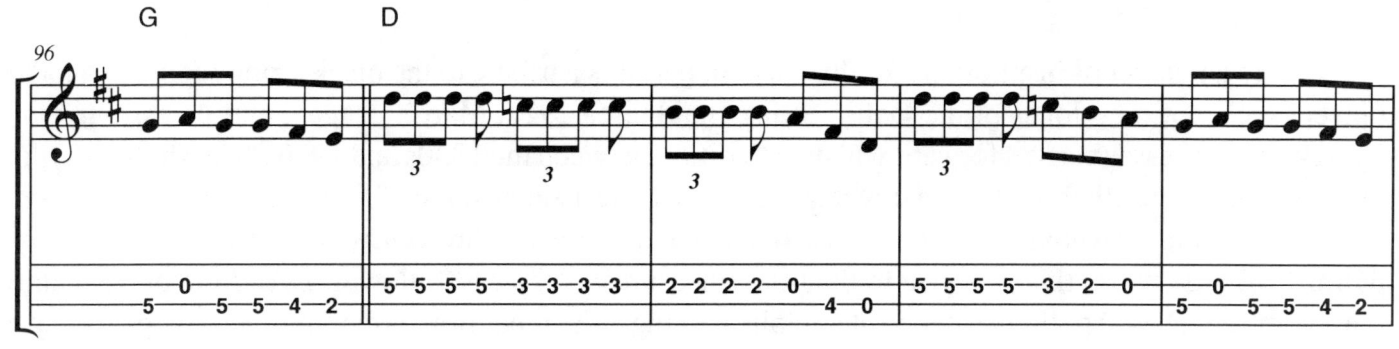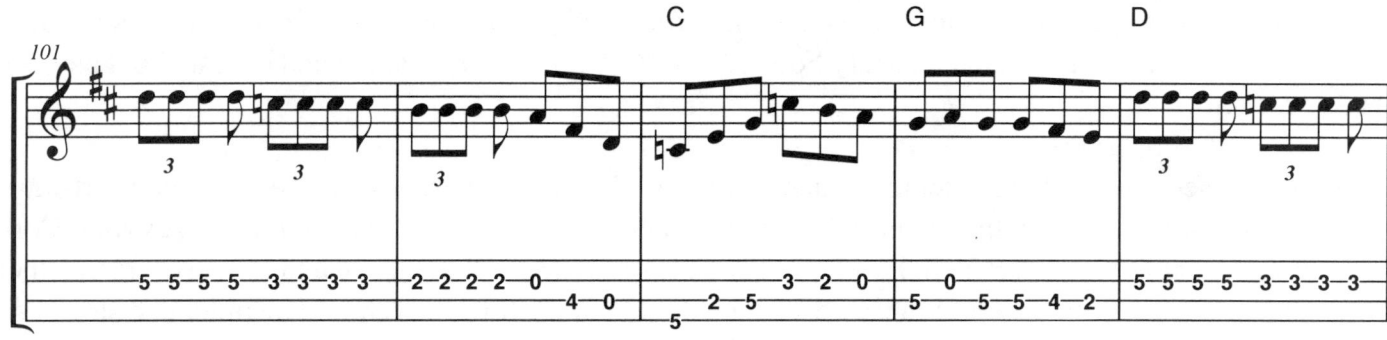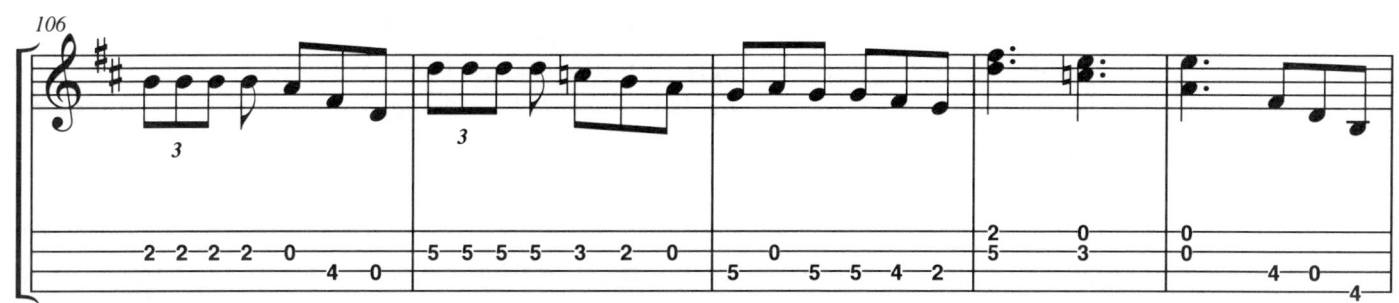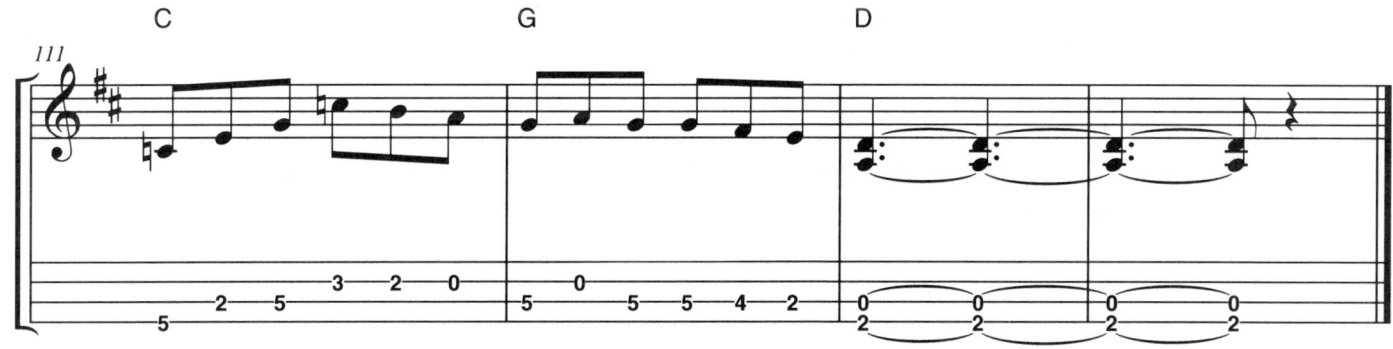

Pizzicato Rag

There were a number of inspirations for this tune. In part it is a tribute to the black string ragtime sound of players such as Coley Jones of the Dallas String Band circa 1927. Martin, Bogan, and Armstrong from Knoxville, Tennessee carried forward with this tradition between the 1930s and 1970s. The shuffle rhythm beginning measure 49, though not a direct quote, is characteristic of some of their tunes, such as *Mexicali Rag*. Another player whose roots lay in East Tennessee, the great Jethro Burns, was an expert in multiple pull-off riffs like those that give rise to the title (measures 17-22 and following). And the player Jethro most admired, Dave Apollon, excelled at complicated rags; the repetition of the first section up an octave, with a glissando back down to the first position sounds like pure Apollon to me. Lastly, the end lick has two melodic lines running contrary to one another. You can hear this basic idea in a lot of fifties guitar playing - at the start of Les Paul and Mary Ford's *How High the Moon*, or at the end of just about any Bill Haley rocker.

Areas that deserve separate practicing include measures 13 and 14, where a double stop is relocated down two frets and repeated, then the D# note is sounded alternately against the adjacent open E string. Continue to hold that D# down through the whole four-note sequence so that the D# and E notes ring together dissonantly. The real fun begins at measure 17. The double pull-off triplets should be practiced slowly so that all three notes become distinct. Work on developing purchase on the strings with your callouses to get a snappy tone. The same idea goes for developing the pull-off licks on the lower strings in later measures. And pay special attention to measures 69-70, where all four fingers have to be set on the first string close together at frets 7, 8, 9, and 10; it's a tight fit, but they should all be set down at one time at the beginning of the sequence. The harmonics in measure 23 are best sounded with the fourth finger - it allows the easiest reach and lightest touch.

The second section starts by repeating the melody an octave higher. It is important when launching into this passage to have worked out the positioning ahead of time. Start at measure 33 with the second finger on the F, 13th fret, then shift position up one fret at the start of measure 35, grabbing the E note, 12th fret with the first finger. Then finger the C note, 15th fret with your second finger, so that when you slide down an octave to make the glissando you will arrive in position.

Note that the guitar accompaniment can stop and resume abruptly at the odd cadences to let the mandolin tricks stand out. Thus the actual chord pattern over measures 7 and 8, for example, could be: C * * * * G7 C / , with "*" meaning quarter rests.

Pizzicato Rag

Dan Gelo

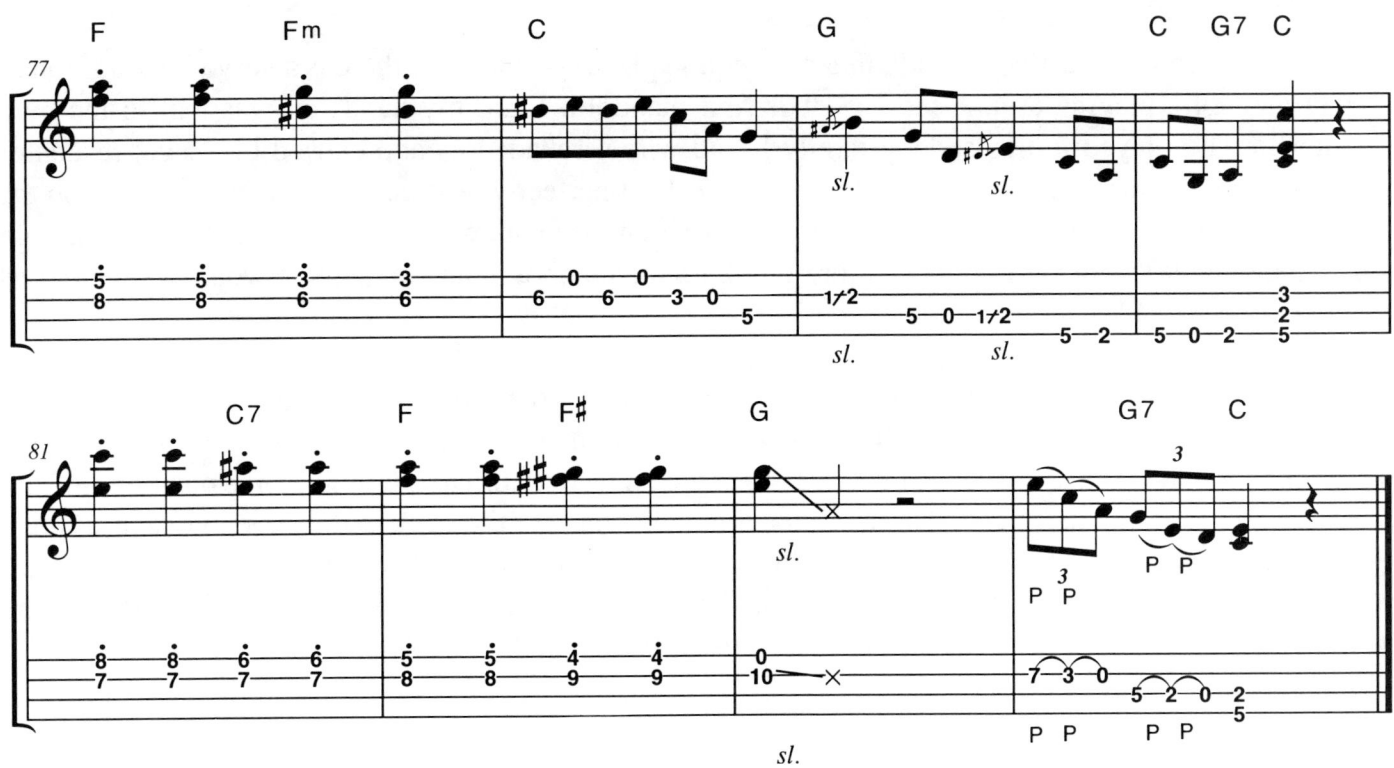

Agrigento

Beyond the stereotypic trilling in godfather movies and pizza commercials there is a very vital tradition of Italian mandolin playing around the U.S. The first mandolin I laid my hands on was lent to me by a gentleman who played in this style, a family friend who serenaded us and carried his Regal resonator mandolin in a canvas bomb-sight cover from a B-17. It fit perfectly. Agrigento is an ancient town on the south coast of Sicily and the home of my grandfather Valentine Gelo, who immigrated to America through Ellis Island in 1905. He passed away before I took up the mandolin but I'm sure he would have enjoyed listening to a tune like this.

The first section is a tarantella, a traditional dance rhythm of southern Italy in 6/8 time. This section forms the basis of the third section, which is just extended with a dramatic cadence. In between is an interlude in a slower tempo in 4/4 that ends with a weird 2/4 meter change to return to 6/8 time. Some position shifting is necessary beginning in measure 16. Bearing in mind that most of the work in the upper passages is done with the first and third fingers, work these climbs and descents out in advance; you'll see that they fall nicely in this key. Almost all the shifts are initiated with the third finger. Tremolo should be added on the sustained chords in the interlude, and can also be used on the quarter notes in the faster sections as a kind of ornamentation.

3

Agrigento

Dan Gelo

Add tremolo freely

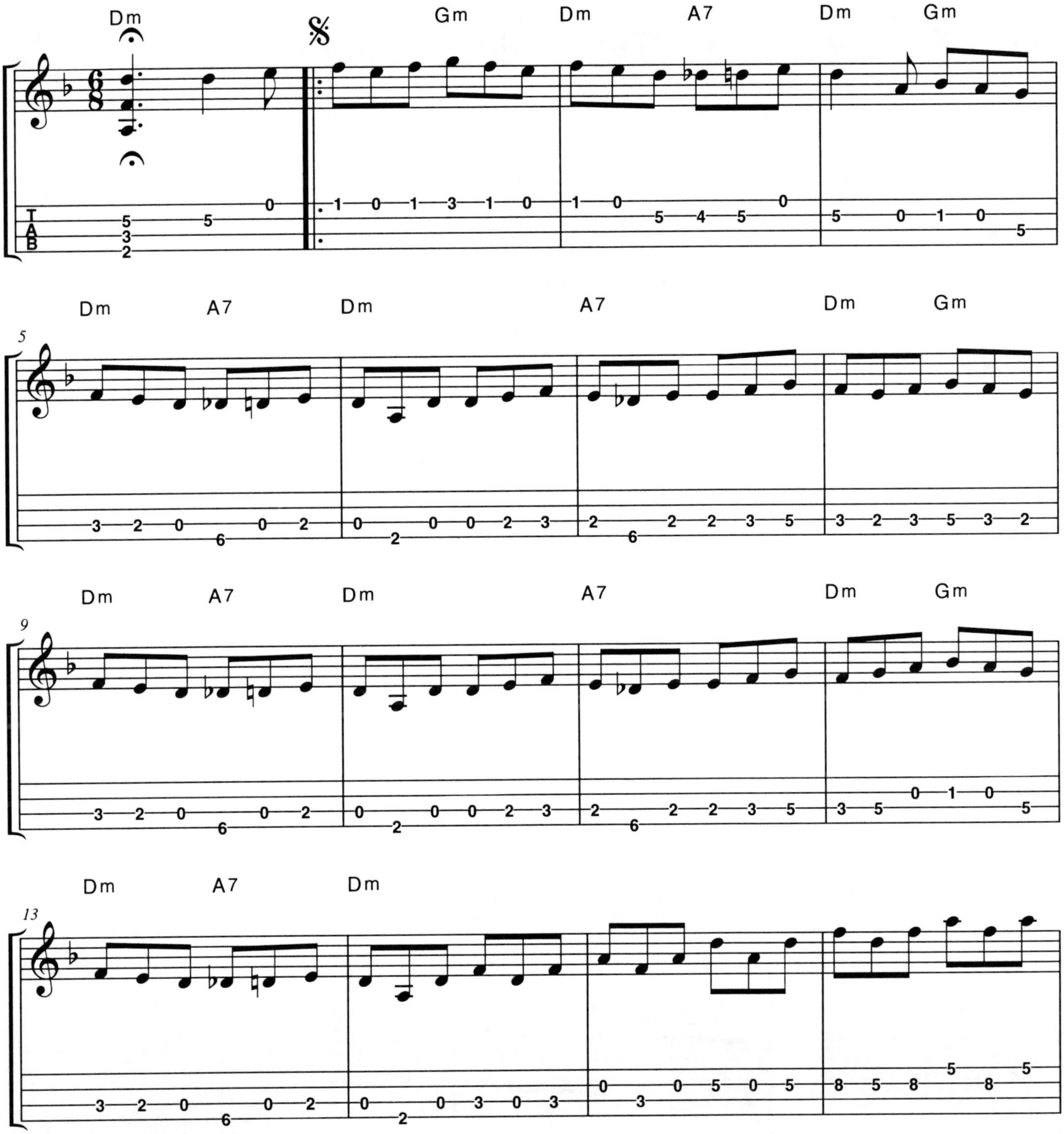

Uncle Dave Medley

Fans of early country music will have to agree that no performer gave us more fun listening that Uncle Dave Macon. Since Uncle Dave had about fifty years' exposure to rural music by the time his recording career began in 1924, listening to him is like stepping back into a nineteenth- century world of hard scrabble farming, river boating, railroading and gambling (these last two activities are the title of one of Uncle Dave's songs). His Fruit Jar Drinkers were a tight band, no pun intended, and their sound had a great texture thanks to the combination of Macon's brisk frailing five-string, the guitar and guitar-banjo of Sam and Kirk McGee, and sweet fiddling by Maizi Todd. Some of my favorite Uncle Dave tunes go together nicely as a medley for solo mandolin: *Tom and Jerry*, *Grey Cat on a Tennessee Farm*, and *Sail Away Ladies*.

The idea here is to take advantage of ringing open strings and also create a loping rhythm, all in order to suggest the sound of old-time fiddle and banjo music. The first two tunes also sound like dulcimer music because of the way the drones alternate between adjacent strings as the melody runs down and up. The three tunes move from the key of A major to D major and then G major. Each of these keys offers open drone strings: A the top two strings, D the third string, and G the bottom two strings, so there is movement throughout the piece from higher to lower drones. Another example of this approach to solo old-time mandolin is Jody Stecher's wonderful version of *Sally Goodin* in *Mel Bay's Master Anthology of Mandolin Solos, Vol. 1*.

Uncle Dave Medley

Dan Gelo

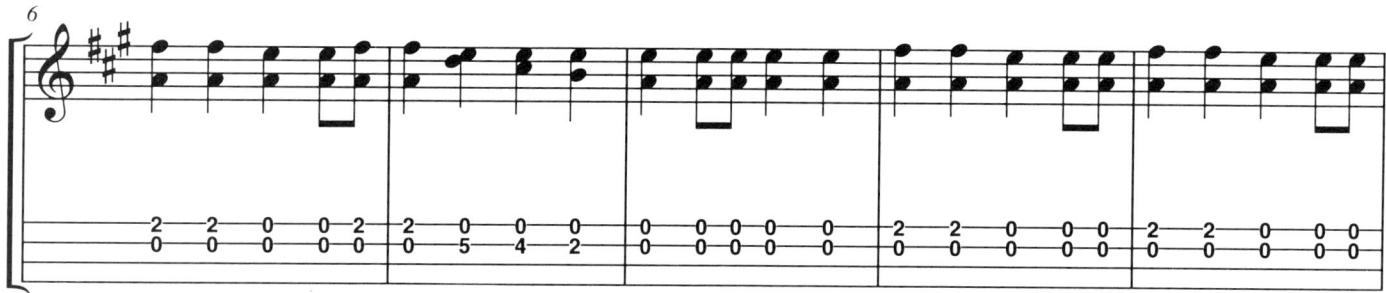

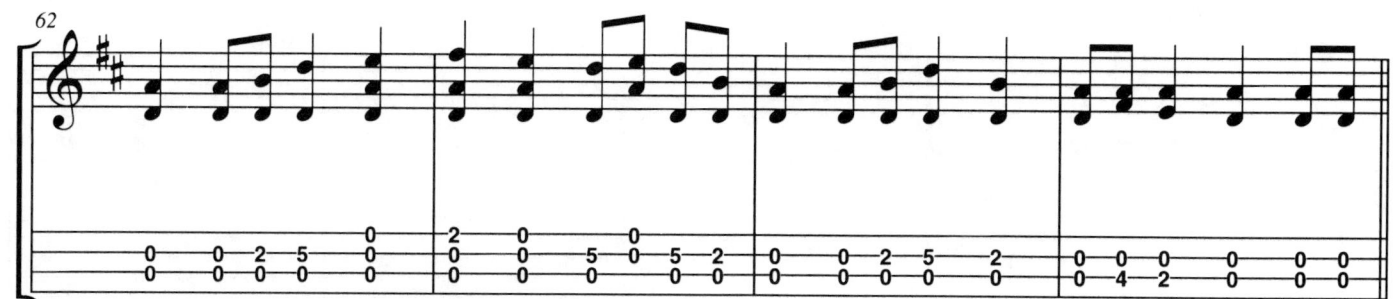
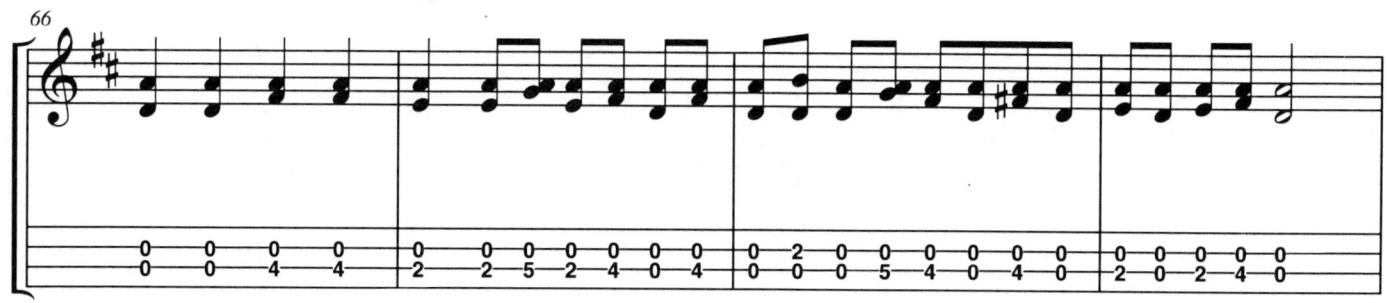
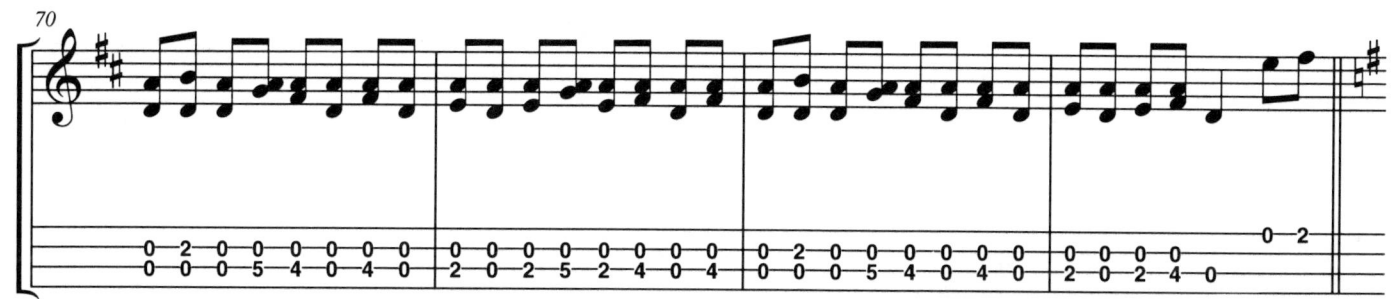

27

Homage to Fauré

I can't say that this piece consciously involves features of the music of the French composer Gabriel Fauré (1845-1924) but it somehow reminded me of the calm and poignant music he was so accomplished at producing. I have fond memories of staying up late to study and write many years ago, and hearing his haunting *Pavanne*, which the classical music station in Philadelphia played every night at midnight. The present composition is more on the order of Fauré's *Berceuse* which, by the way, makes a great mandolin piece.

The most unusual aspect of this piece is the abrupt time signature change at bars 47 and 94. Another notable feature is the introduction of cross-picking when the entire melody is repeated a second time. The key of E major, even with the modulation to F# minor, works beautifully against a rotating pick pattern. Like a lot of effective cross-picking patterns, this one has the strong beats of the melodic rhythm falling at different spots in the six-note rotation of the pattern. The tempo throughout should be pretty brisk.

5

Homage to Fauré

Dan Gelo

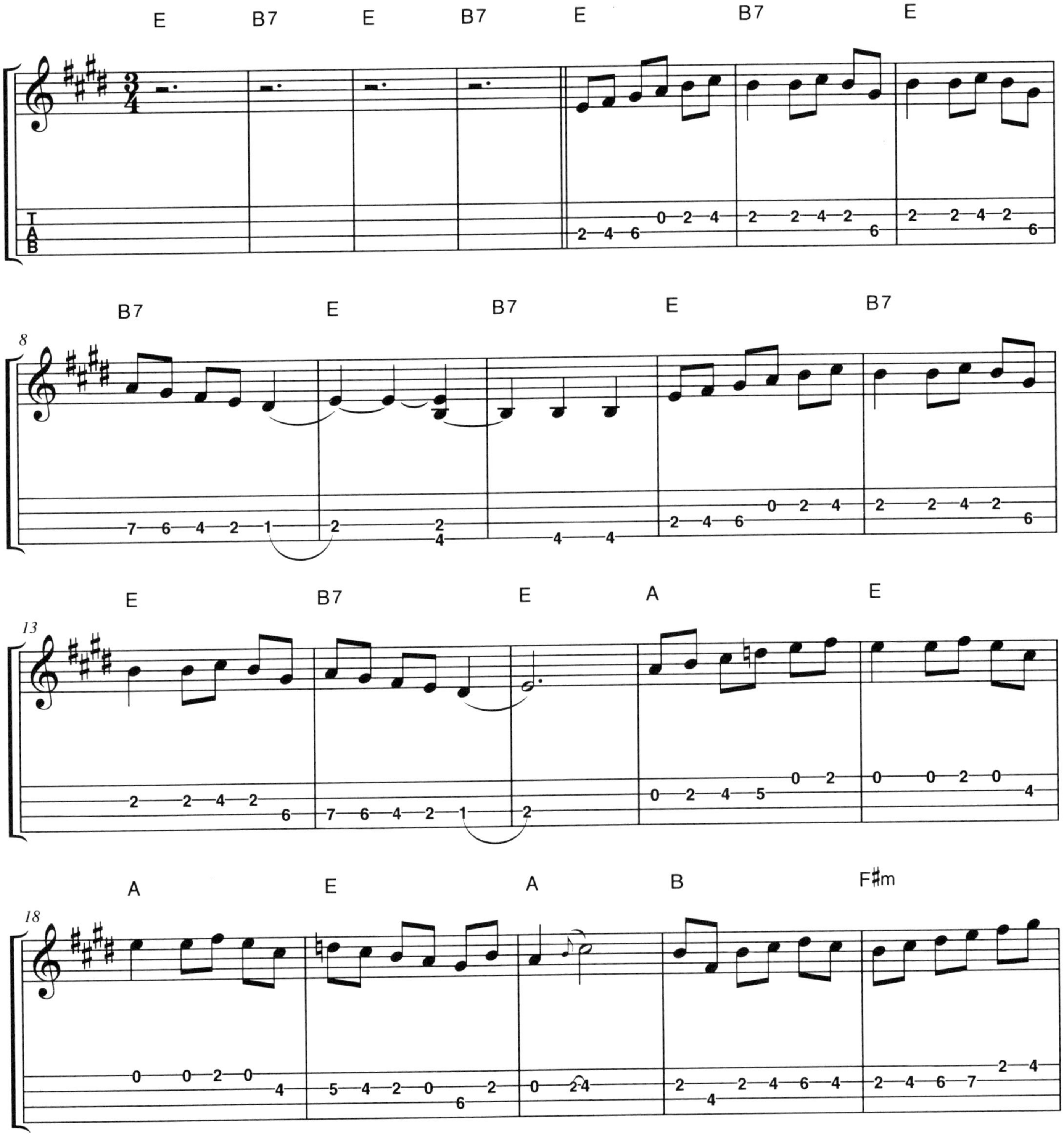

Southern Railroad Locomotive Blues

When Bill and Charlie Monroe hit the radio show circuits of the midwest and southeast in 1934 there was nobody like them. Earlier, mandolinists in country music were used to supplying plunky turn-arounds between the verses of sentimental songs. The smooth but driving, lightning-fast mandolin and guitar we almost take for granted today must have been stunning to folks hearing the Monroe Brothers for the first time. That sound was on my mind when this tune came out, and I wrote it to be short so it would sound like one of the intros or outros on the old radio shows, but of course it can be extended with more repetitions.

Chugging trains, bucking mules, and foxhounds barking are some of the programmatic effects customary in southern string band music. This song contains uncanny train sound effects that will amaze your friends. Well, not really, but there are some train sounds suggested in the opening bars and further along. In the Monroe style the left hand is pretty much subordinated to what the right hand is doing, so the rapid tremoloing of the double stops is the most important element of the tune, and the melody doesn't have to be precise, just supportive of the driving effect. Also in this style, the third and seventh scale tones are "blue notes" that can be major or minor. Some of this ambiguity is built into the melody, but try also substituting F# for F natural in measure 32.

Southern Railroad Locomotive Blues

Dan Gelo

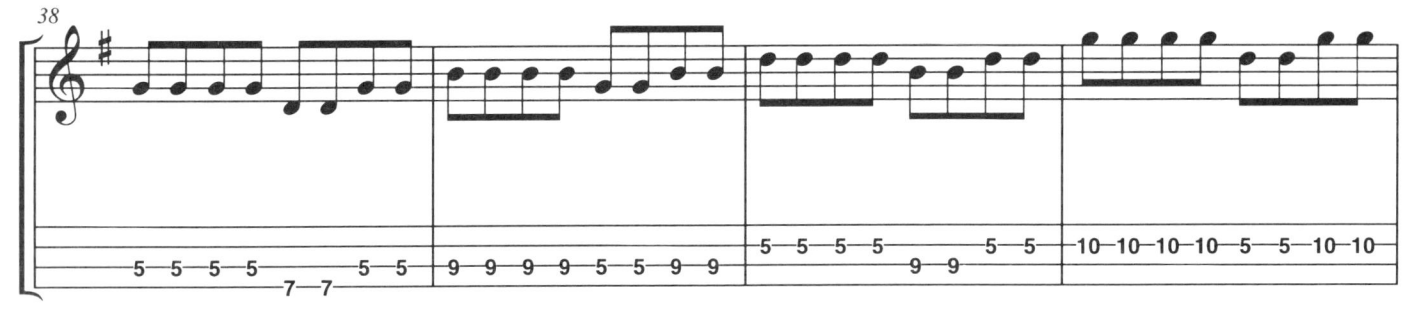
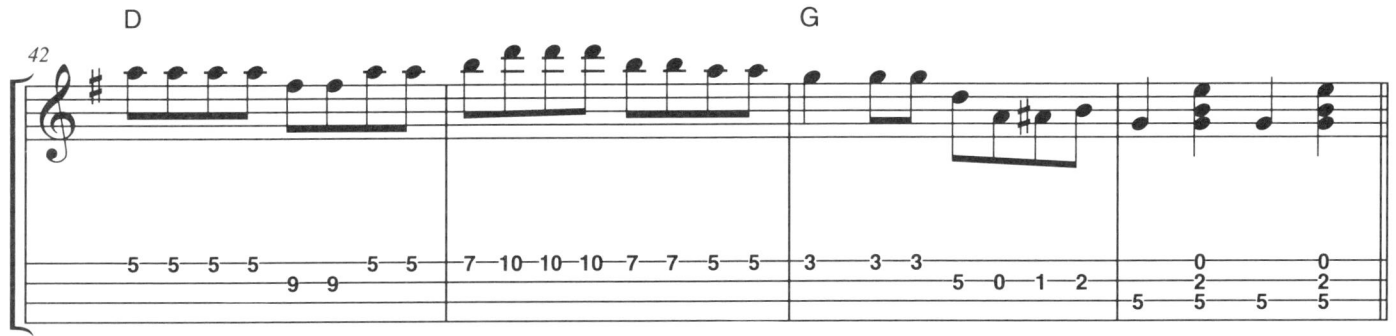
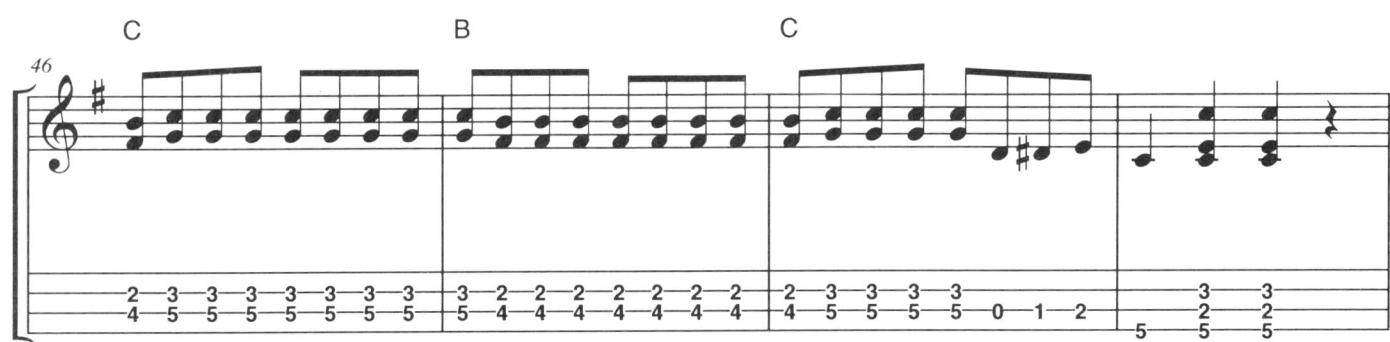
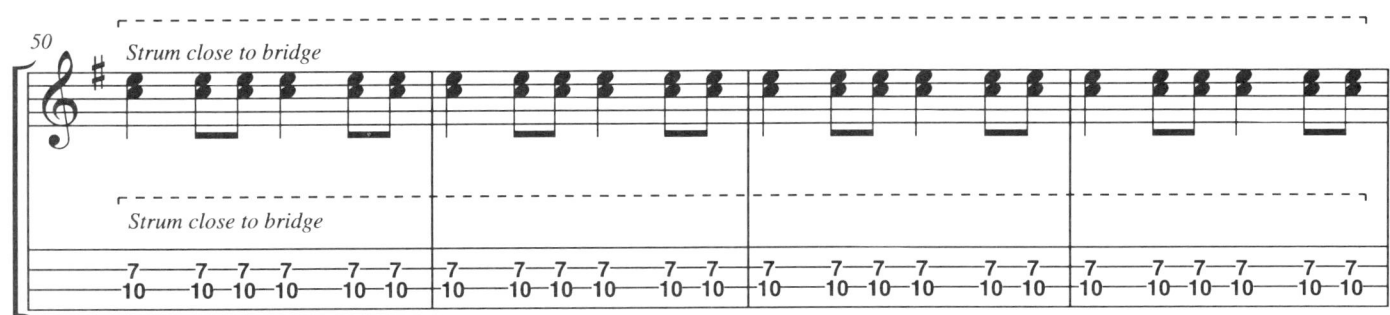
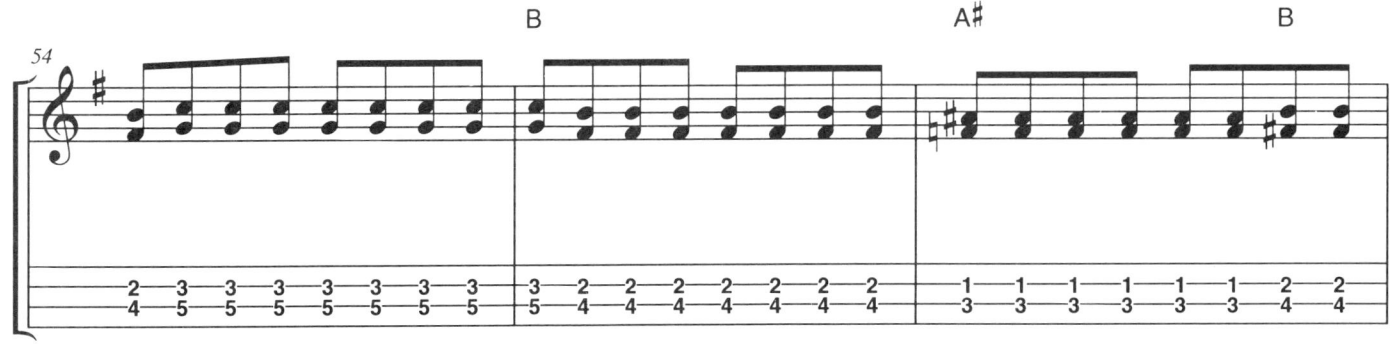

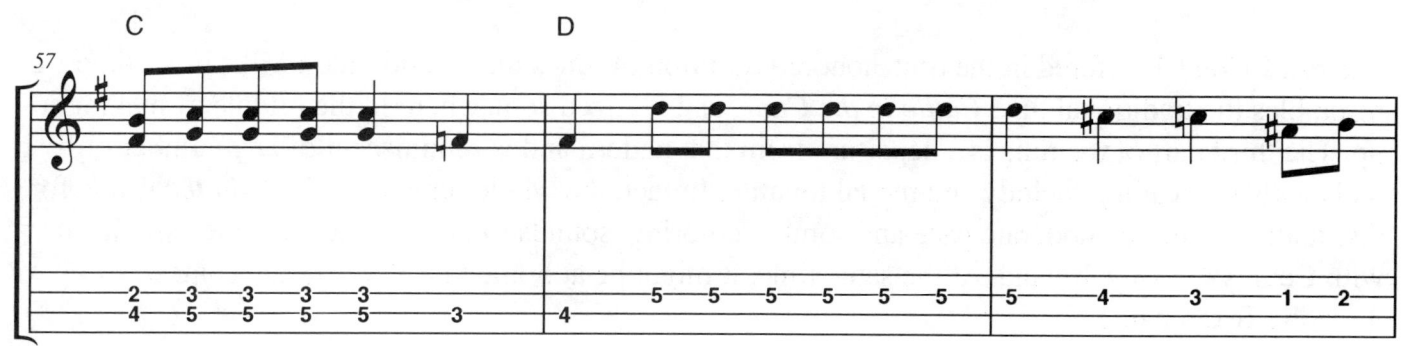

39

Maverick Creek

Maverick Creek is offered in the time honored tradition of tunes that sound kind of like other tunes. It resembles the traditional tune *Cattle in the Cane*, as I realized somewhere in the middle of making it up. The third part of the tune is a departure from that pattern and is reminiscent of any number of Irish reels with a cascading melody and modal tonality. In fact, the whole tune (and *Cattle in the Cane*, for that matter), with its moderate pace and somber coloring, sounds to my ear like the style associated with County Galway, Ireland. At the same time, it might be at home in a Texas fiddle contest, so I gave it a good Texan name.

The tune is not too difficult to finger since all the notes are in the first position. The only part that is a bit unusual for this kind of instrumental is the change from the key of G major in the third section to A minor in the fourth section (which is basically the first section reiterated). Thus in the second ending of the third section (measures 25-26) the melody successively outlines the D minor and E major chords, repeating the same pattern, only two tones higher the second time, walking up to the A note in measure 27. Double-stops in measure 35 add a little extra to the melody for variation, and the resolving phrase is repeated a little differently to form an ending (measures 41- 44).

7

Maverick Creek

Dan Gelo

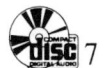

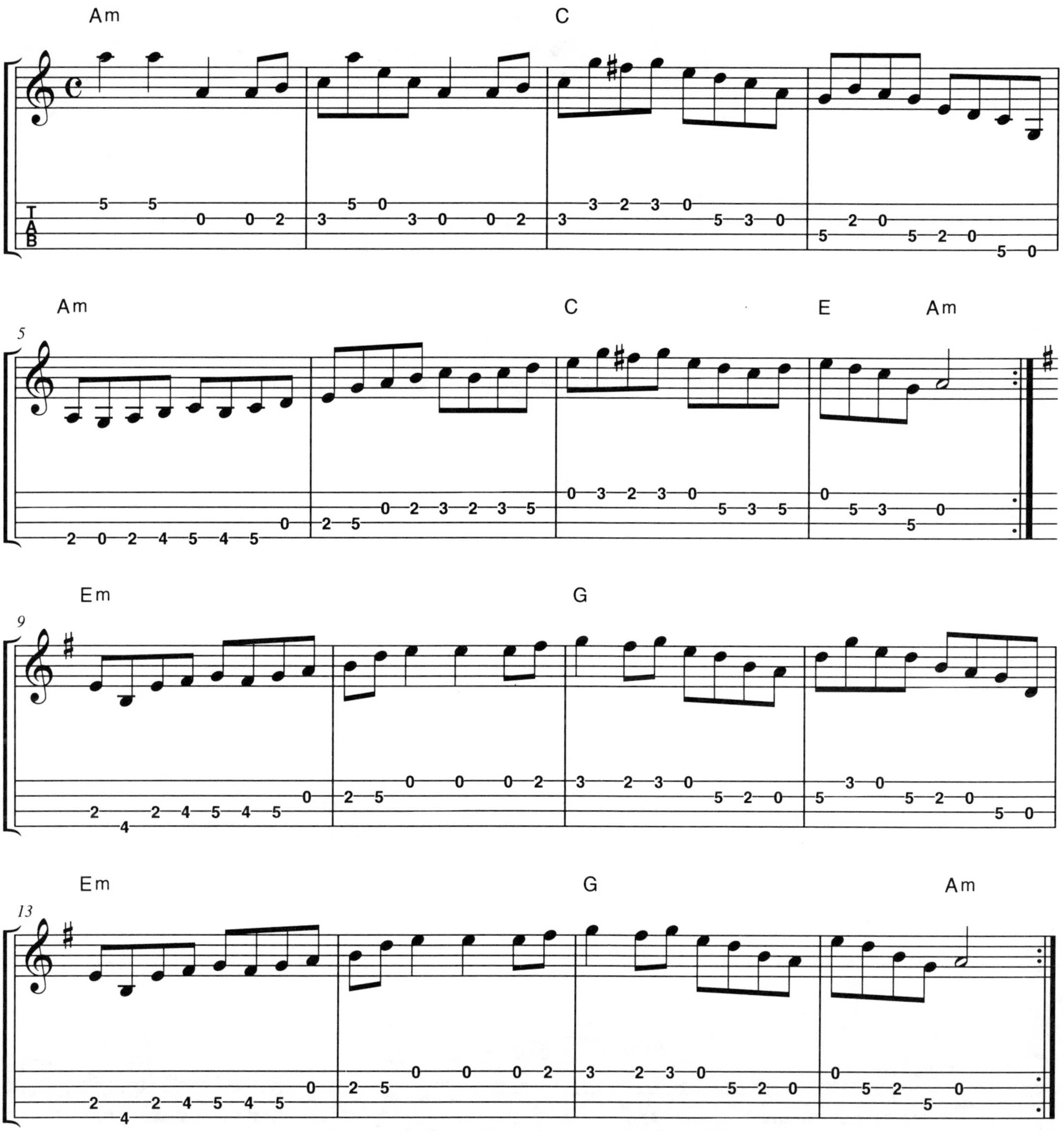

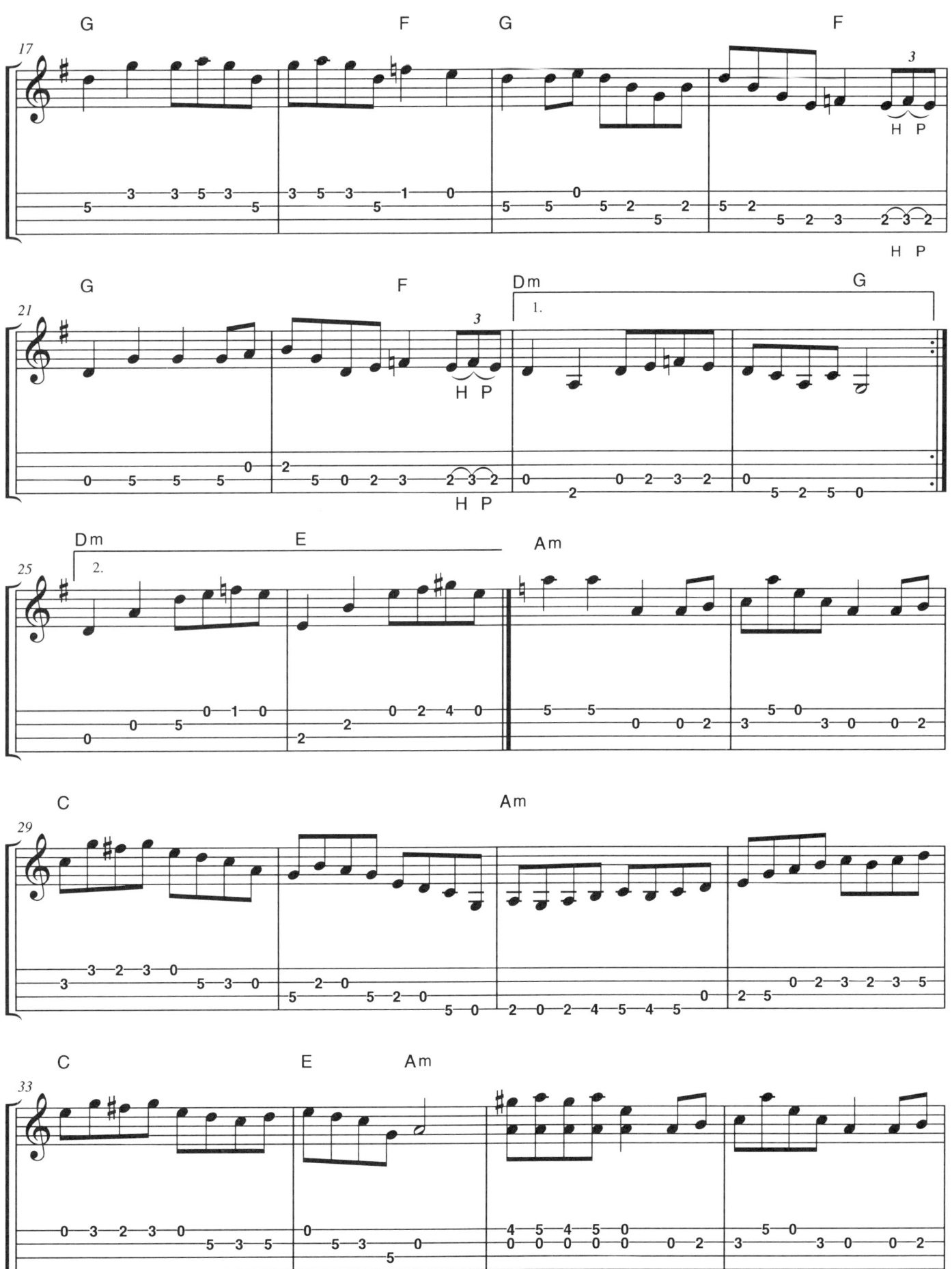

Angel Dance

In looking at the great classical mandolin pieces I am always amazed by the understanding of the fretboard that is evident in these compositions. The Beethoven sonatinas and the works by Mozart and Hummel appear as if written by devoted mandolin players; the position shifts and cross-picking patterns fit the instrument exactly. The chords and picking pattern in Mozart's *Canzonetta No. 16* from *Don Giovanni* - one of the great moments in mandolin melody - inspired the tune *Angel Dance*. This piece originally appeared in *Mel Bay's Master Anthology of Mandolin Solos, Vol. 1*.

Angel Dance

Dan Gelo

Raritan Ride

The mid to late 1970s was a great time for mandolin playing with superb players like Doyle Lawson and Jimmy Gaudreau turning out original tunes and arrangements of standards that tastefully extended the boundaries of bluegrass. *Raritan Ride* is a tune from those days in a newgrass vein. Like a fiddle tune, the tune is structured basically in two parts. The hammer-ons played against open strings in the second part of the tune are similar to what is done sometimes when Telecaster® players imitate steel guitar pedal work.

Jethro Burns called these "Cramer licks" after Floyd Cramer, the country pianist who made his career on the slip-note style. As the entire tune is repeated the first section starts off an octave lower than before, and the second section has hammers that are different than before. The hammer licks can be worked on separately, tried in different places on the fretboard, and put into other tunes.

Raritan Ride

Dan Gelo

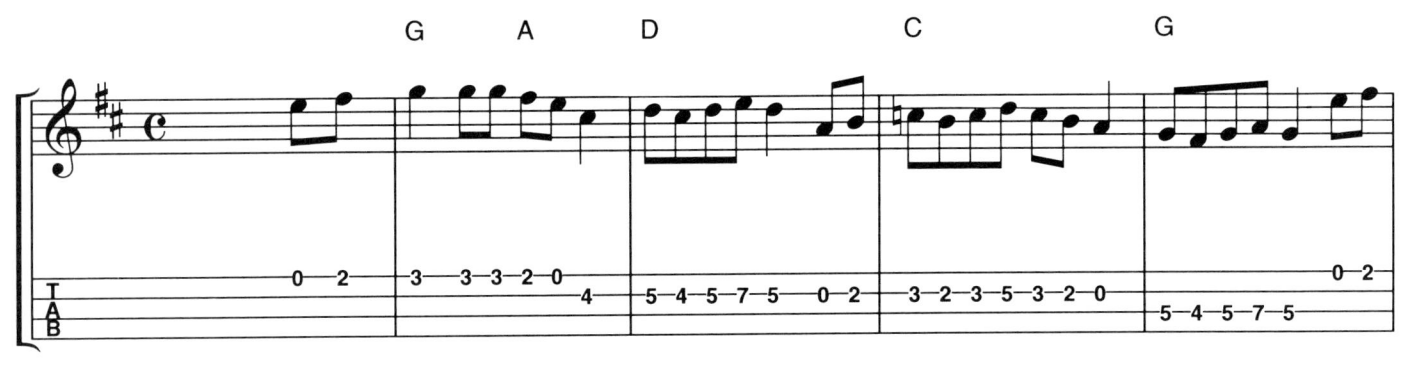
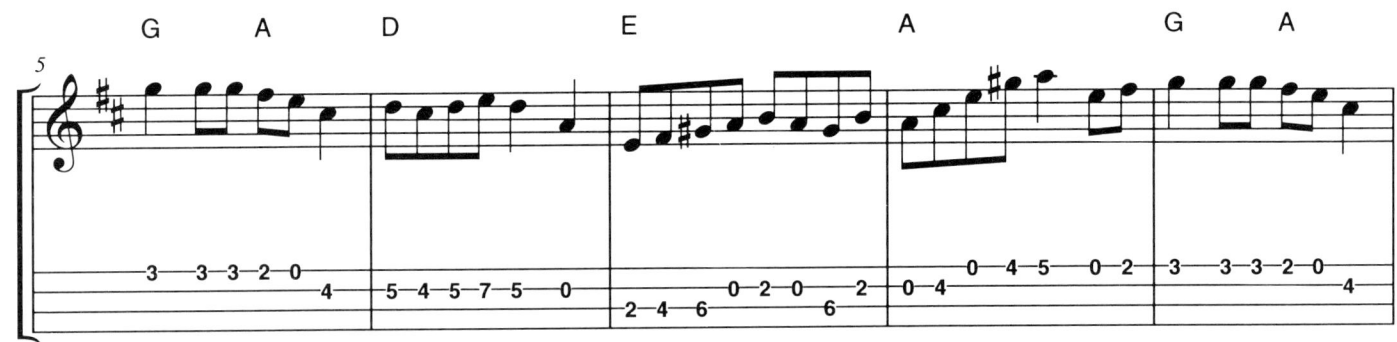
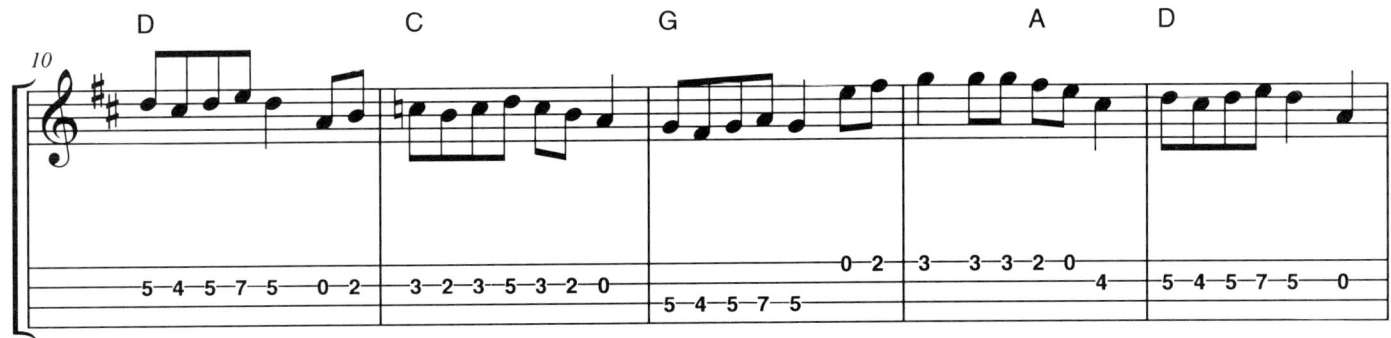
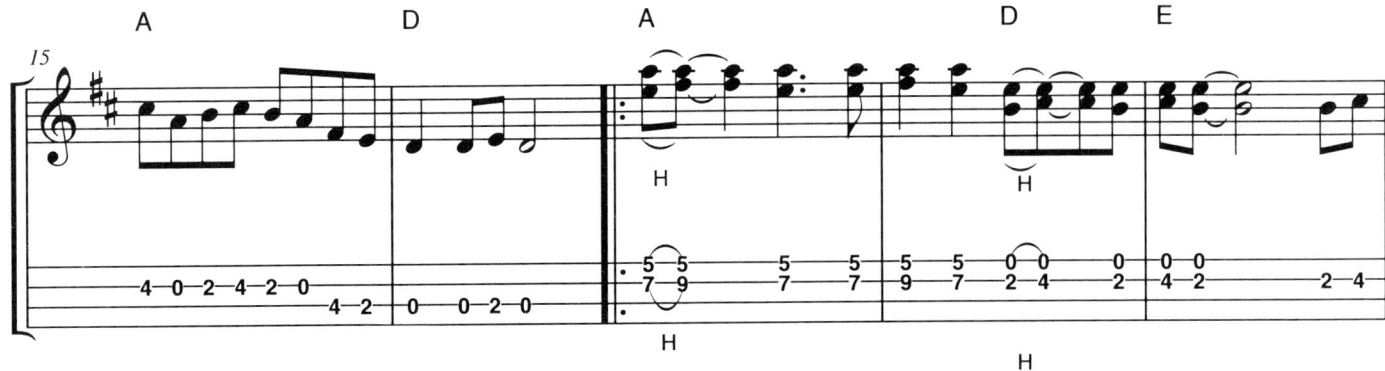

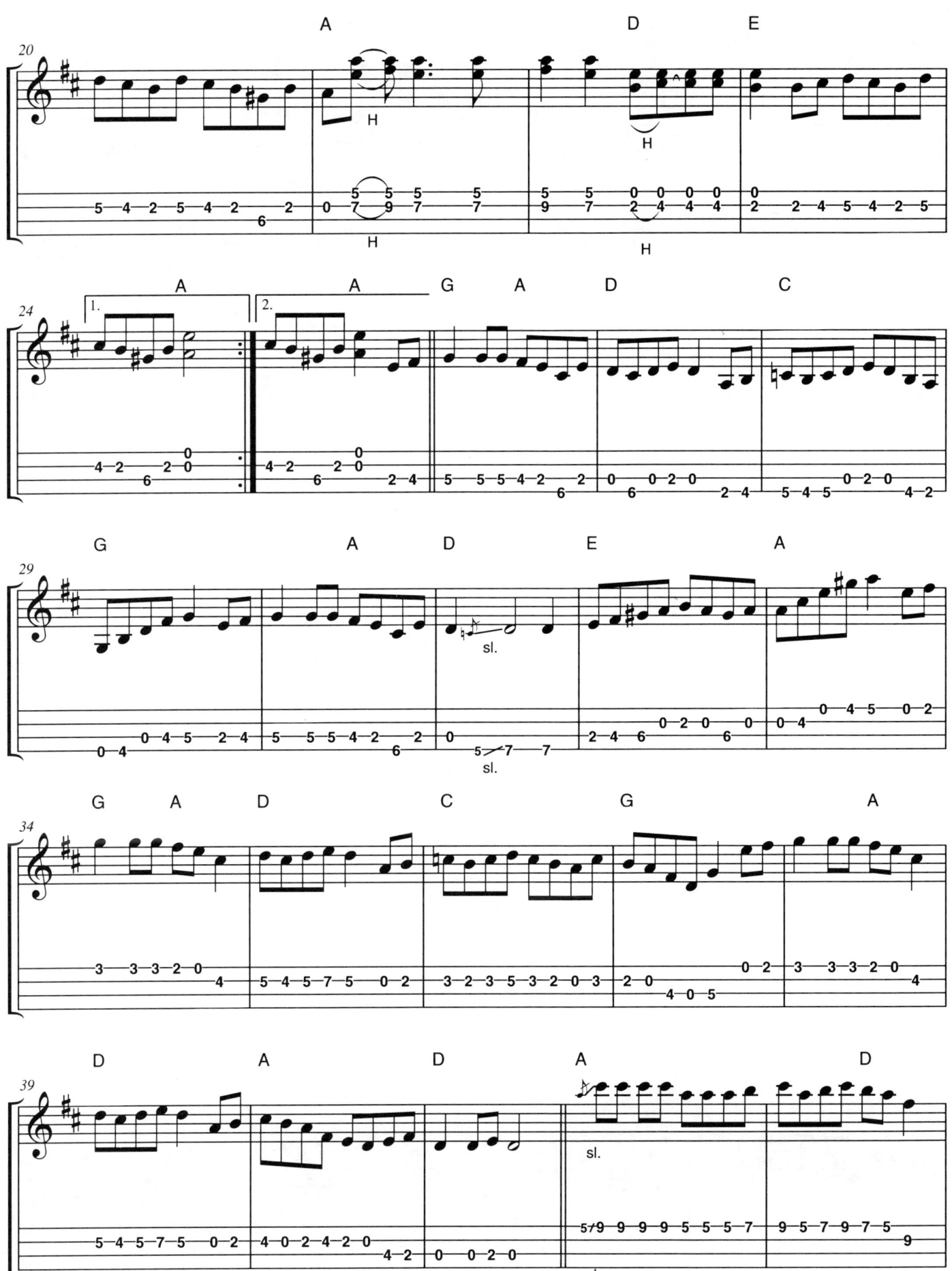

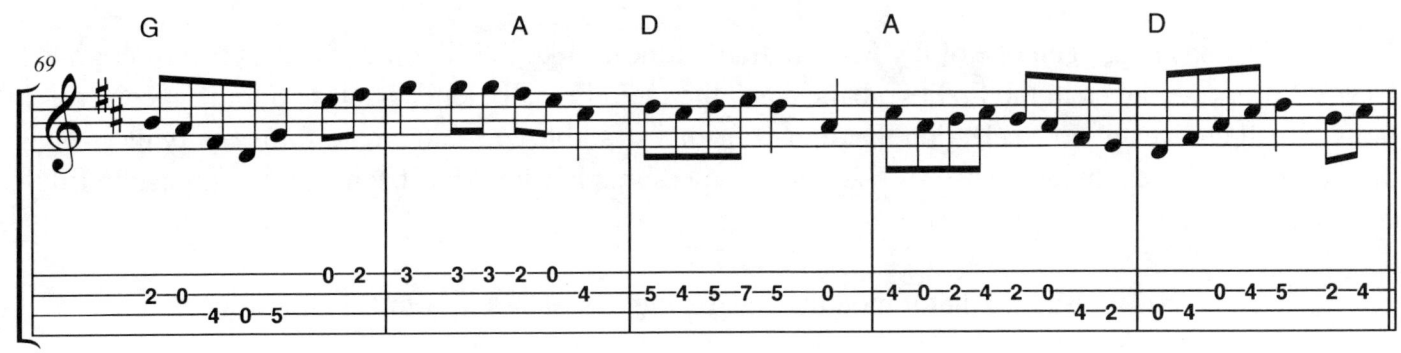

Miller's Reel

Miller's Reel has long been one of my favorite fiddle tunes. I like the way the chords move through the I-IV-V-I progression, as in the first two bars. Also, the melody really lends itself to a lot of nice variations. Small choices in note selection that depart from a straight scale can create some really nice tonalities (see, for example, measures 6 and 53). I guess this is why it has been a popular piece in fiddle contests.

This arrangement is unusual in that it modulates from the key of A major to E major. I haven't heard the tune played that way by anybody else, but it seemed like a natural thing to try. A good deal of the fingering can just shift over one course. The only tricky part comes when the melody runs against the F# and B chords. Here you need to do a little position shifting. In measures 45 and 53 position your left hand with the first finger at the fourth fret, and in measures 51-52 and 58-59 the first finger needs to be moved to the first fret. Otherwise the fingering is not too tough, standard for A and E major, first finger at the second fret. There are a few nice hammered triplets and an end tag. To extend the tune for performance, the first entire pass of the tune in the key of A can be repeated before going to E.

A version of *Miller's Reel* for flatpicked guitar (key of A major) appears in my book *Mel Bay's Fiddle Tunes and Irish Music for Guitar.*

Miller's Reel

Traditional
arr. Dan Gelo

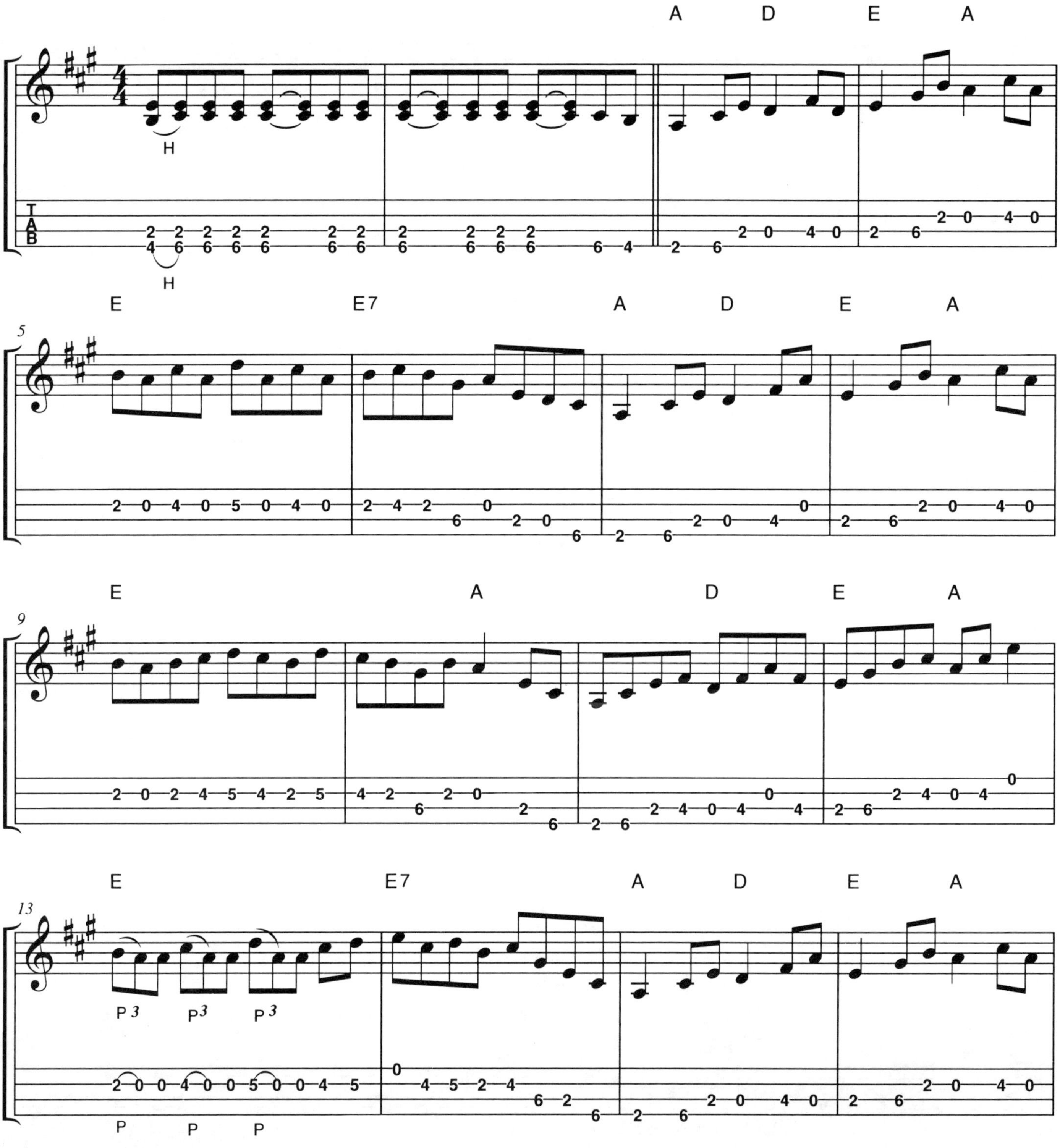

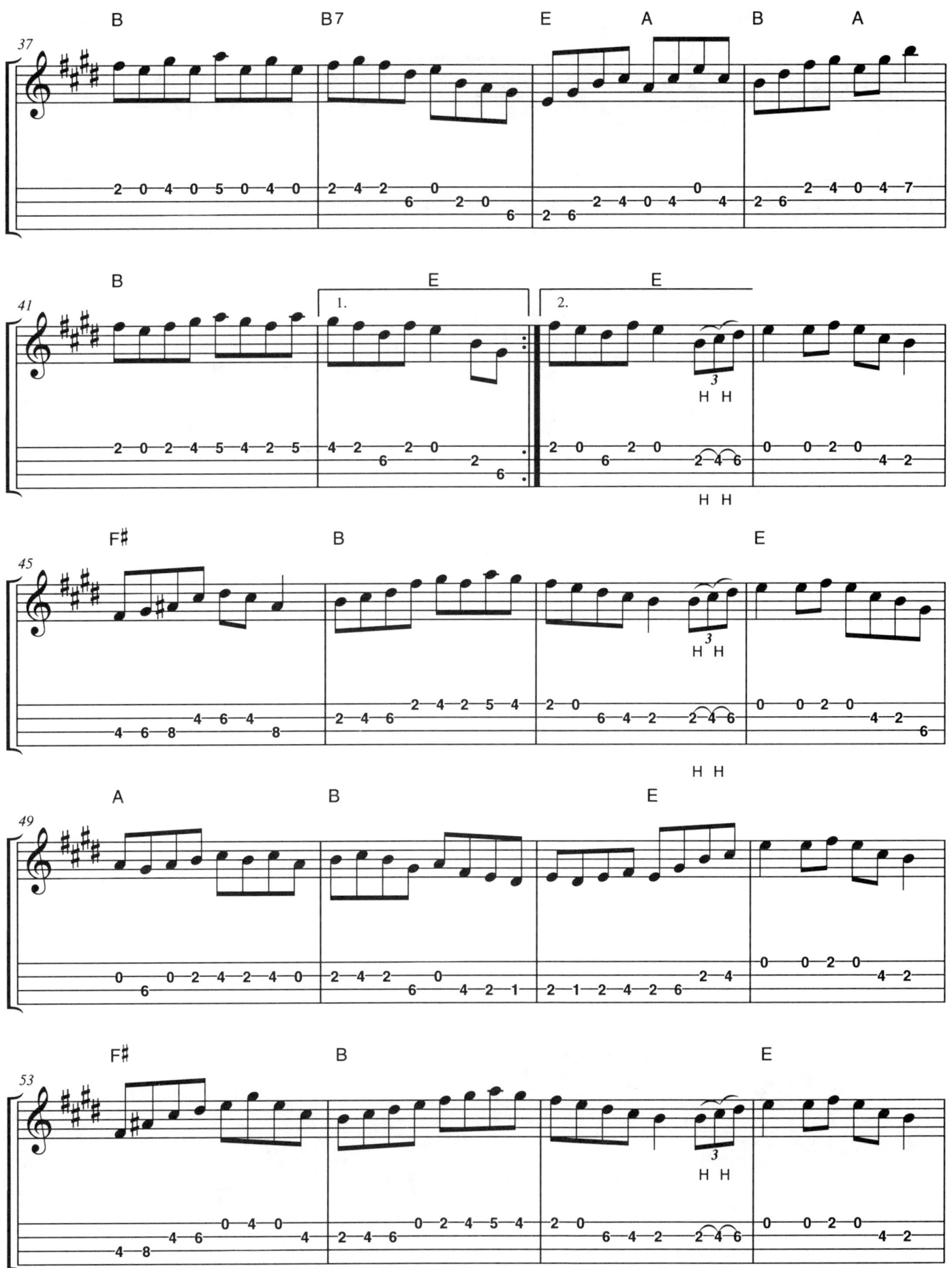

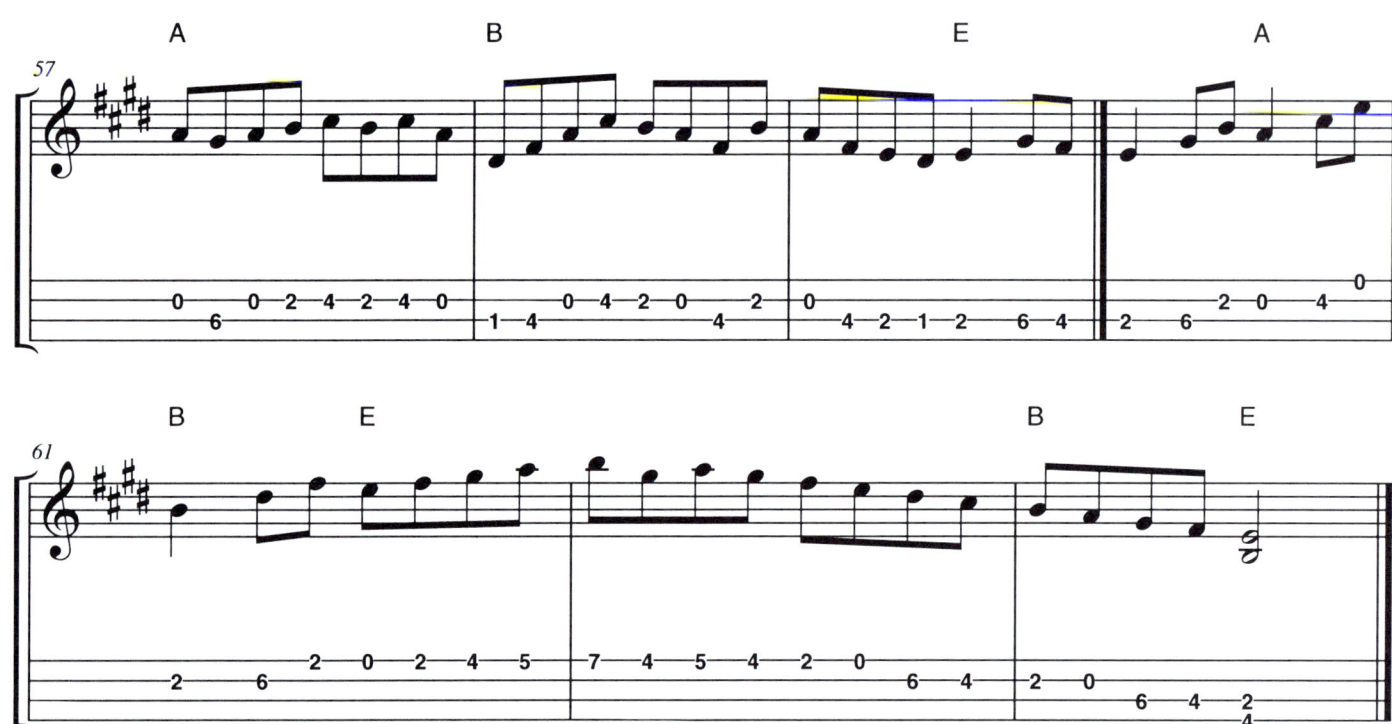

Double-Talkin' Blues

Blues tunes like this one sound great on electric mandolin, and I like to play this on my 1960 Gibson Florentine electric solid body. Mine is kind of beat up but it's loud, the Les Paul model of the mandolin world, and no banjo can drown it out!

The tune is based on a common primitive blues turnaround used by fingerpicking guitarists. Instead of just showing up at cadences, the turnaround figure becomes the main melody, played in the initial tonic (measures 1 and 2) and the subdominant (measures 5-6) as well as the phrase endings (measures 11-12, for example). Between the first and second double bars, a descending single-string lick replaces the opening pattern for variety's sake. Past the second double bars, another variation kicks off with adjacent double stops walked down and up the first and second courses. Further along a similar idea, but on the low strings, forms measures 37-40. Another distinctive move involves sequences of double stops in which one voice remains stationary and the other walks to establish a boogie riff; this move too is performed on the high strings (measures 29-30) and the low strings (measures 41-44).

Double-Talkin' Blues

Dan Gelo

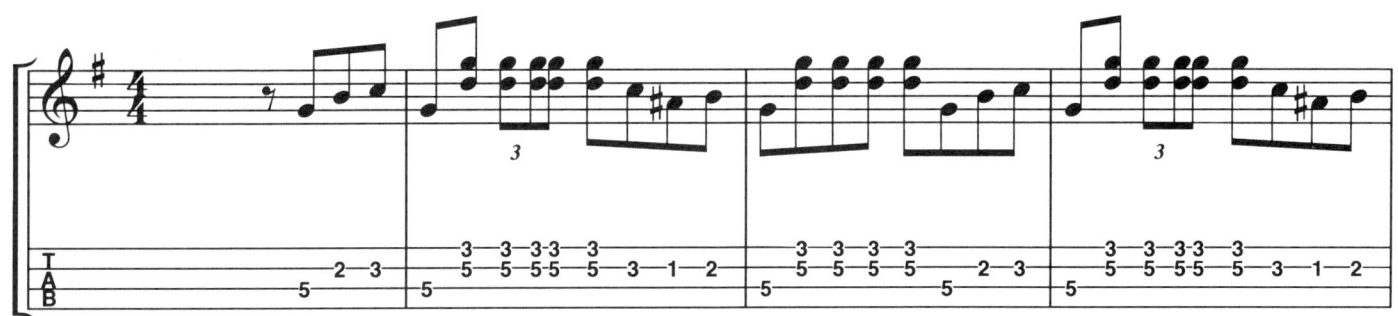
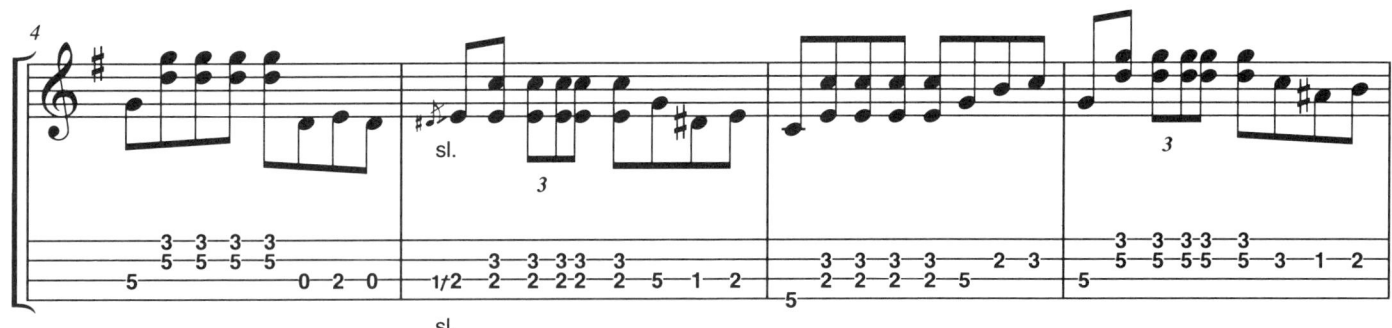
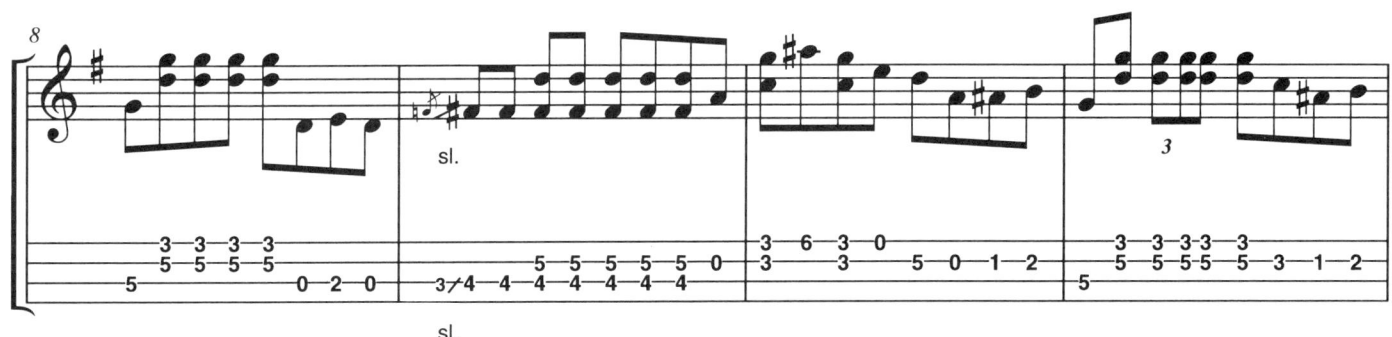
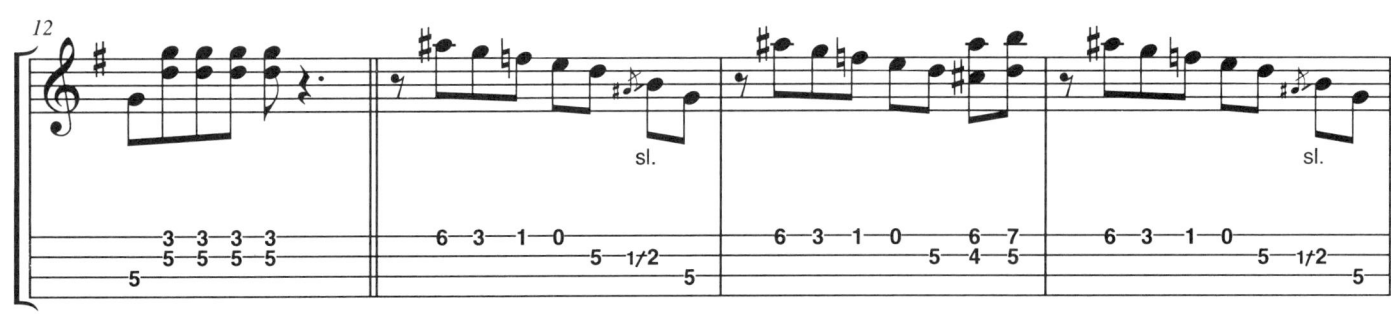

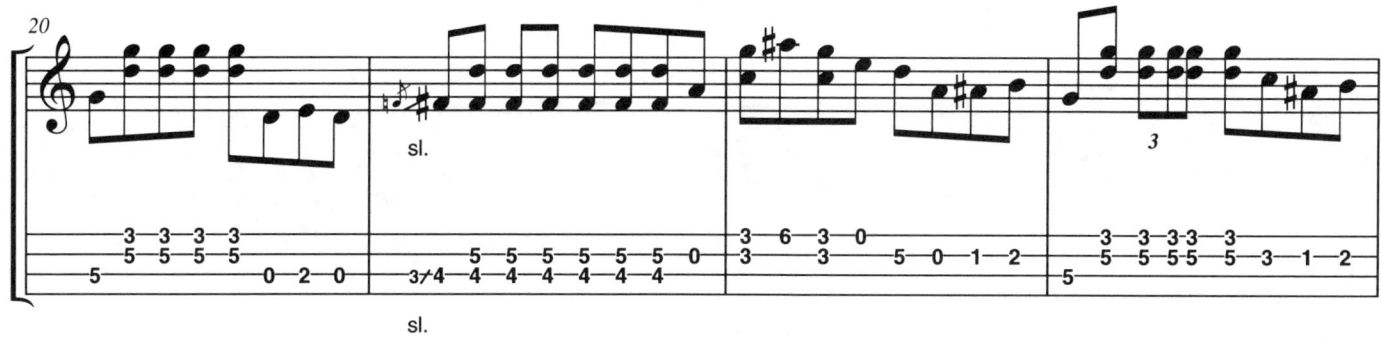

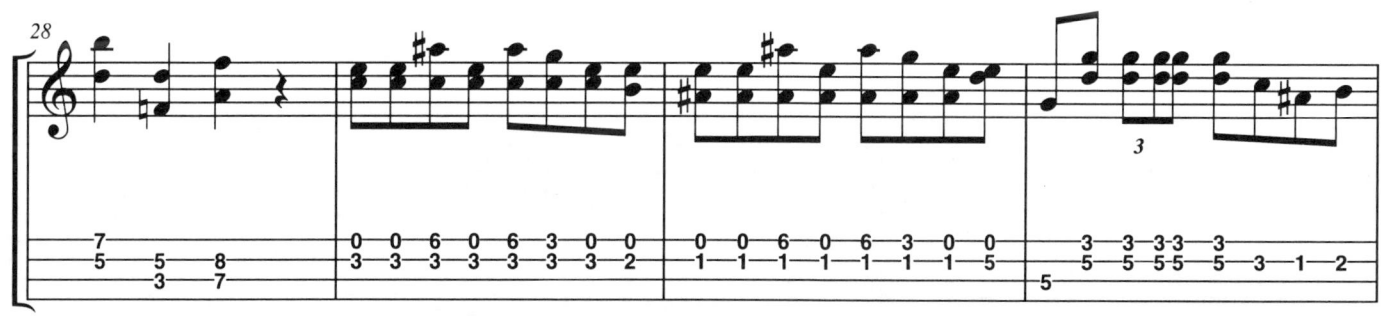
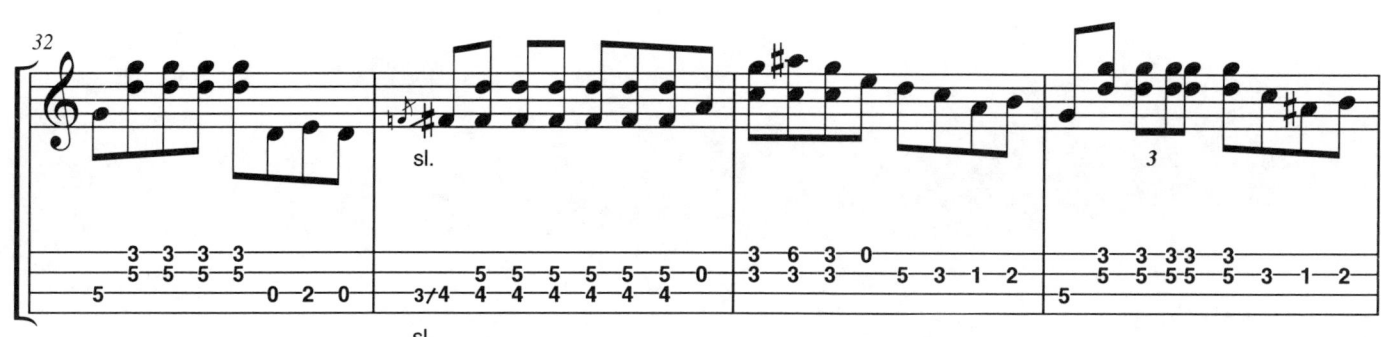

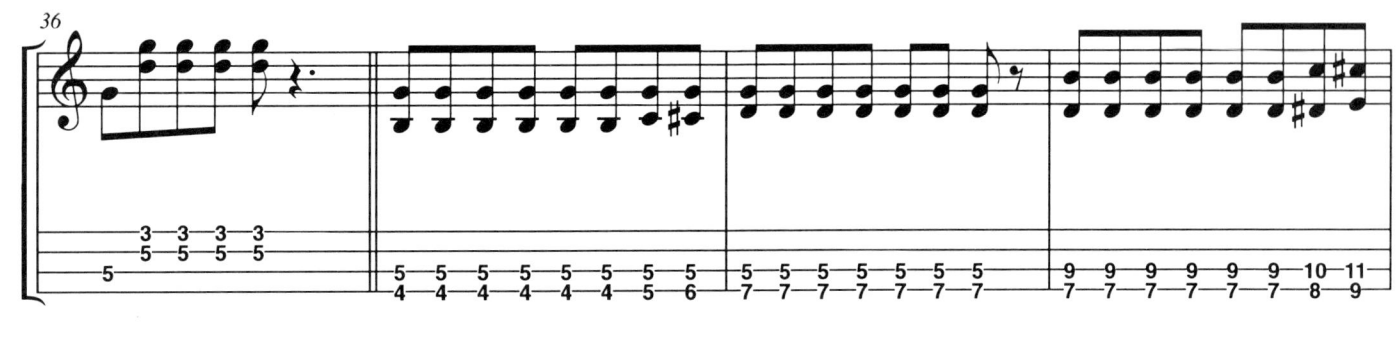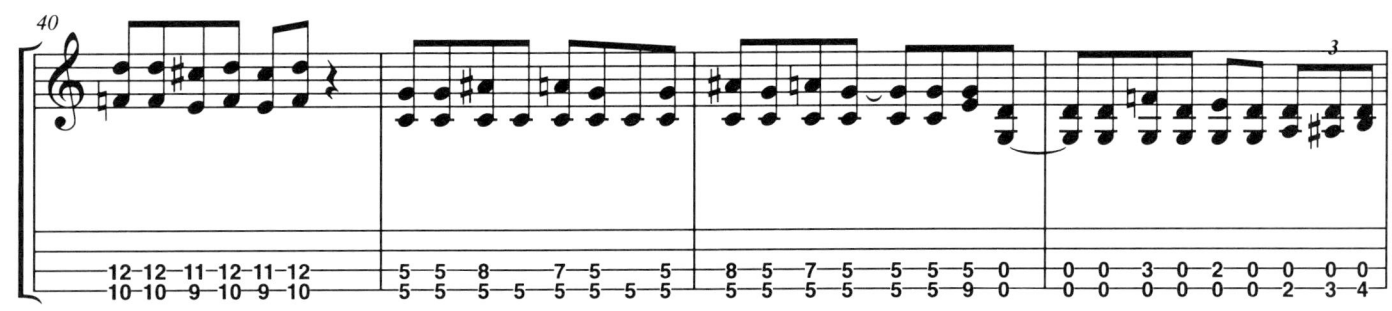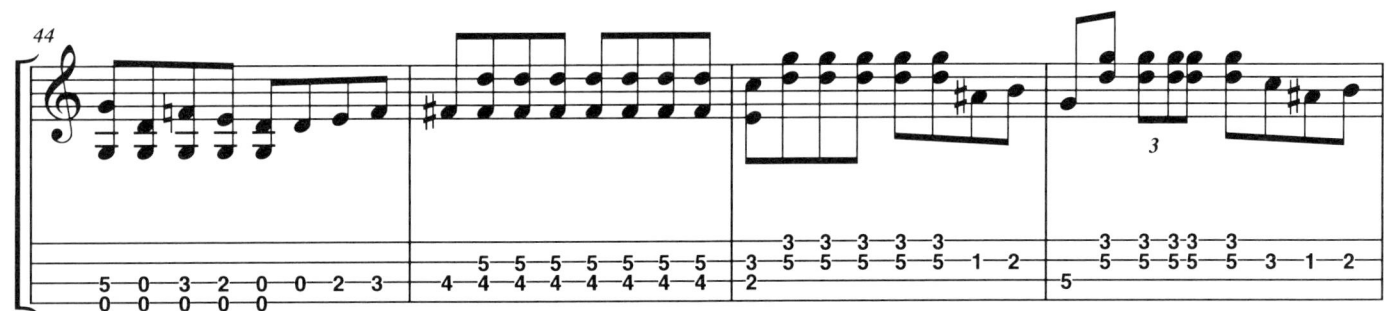

Big Sciota

Over the past few years *Big Sciota* has become a popular tune in parking-lot jams at bluegrass festivals. It's a good old traditional fiddle tune, probably of northern origin. It shows up in West Virginia and northward as far as Canada and is often played as a contra dance tune.

Some folks have speculated that "Sciota" is a corruption of "Scotia," as in Nova Scotia, and concluded therefore that the tune is of Canadian origin. I always imagined that the tune came from around south central Ohio, where the Scioto River flows, not far from West Virginia. The place name Scioto or Sciota is also found in northeastern Pennsylvania and in Illinois. All of these places were occupied by the migratory Shawnee Indians, and Scioto appears to be derived from the Shawnee village name Sonniato. I think, then, that the tune, or its title at least, originated in Ohio or maybe in Pennsylvania.

In an effort to keep things interesting there is a statement of the opening phrase one octave below (starting measure 33); here you kind of run out of mandolin so you have to compress the melody a little. The same basic idea is restated differently yet again starting at measure 65 by using the normal metric pattern of the notes with different tones. Measure 57 uses a quick, syncopated sequence of descending notes that are actually broken double stops. This trick is followed by a descending pattern of high notes alternating with the open first course in measures 61 and 62. Try pulling off on the fretted notes in this sequence for more emphasis if you like.

12

Big Sciota

Traditional arr. Dan Gelo

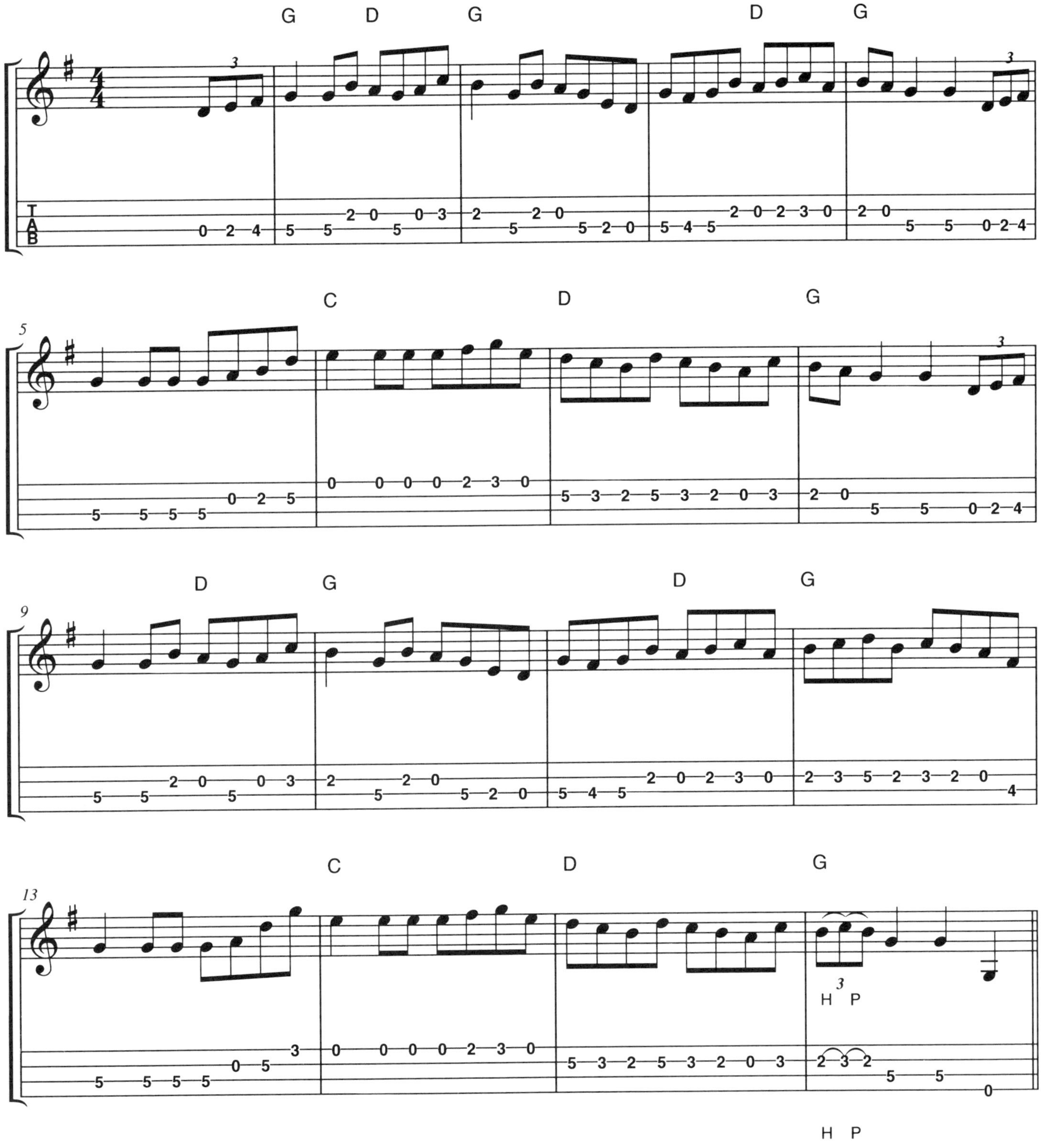

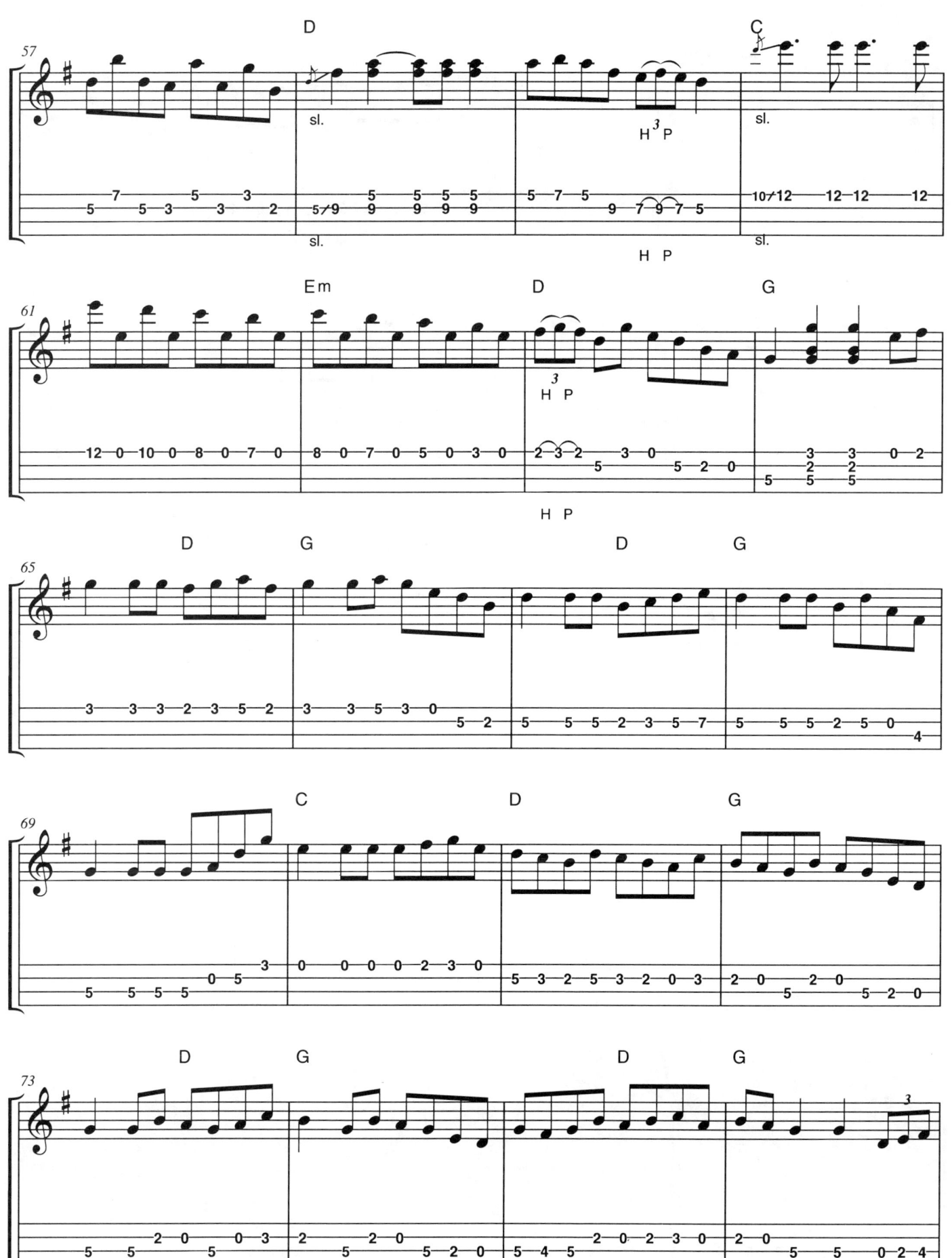

Jethritis

Many of us were exposed to this infectious condition while watching Homer and Jethro do their great parody tunes on the old TV variety shows ("If you electrocute me, I want to hold your hand..."). I caught an incurable case upon hearing the mandolin solo on The Country Fiddlers' recording of *Mississippi Sawyer.** Jethro Burns was the one who showed a lot of us mandolin players that (with all due respect to the Father of Bluegrass) there was more to life than *Rawhide*. He could play it all superbly, but to my mind he was at his best on ragtime and swing numbers such as those he recorded with Chet Atkins. Jethritis is an attempt to capture some of that style and excitement.

The tune is set up in three parts: a theme, improvisation, and return to the theme again but using double stops. Note that a lot of the double stops fall on an upstroke (as in measure 8), and that is how they should be sounded, with the higher note struck before the lower one. The second ending of the first section is an optional way of adding syncopation. No Jethro tribute would be complete without some quick quotes, so you'll see a snippet of classical melody in measures 26 and 27, the same one Jethro used to drop into Chet's *Main Street Breakdown*, and also a little bit of *Dixie* (measures 44-45) as a nod to Jethro's home turf. Moving among the double stops in measures 50-53 can get a little confusing so it will be worthwhile to practice adjusting your finger spacing in order to grab these accurately. Another contrary motion end lick similar to the one used in *Pizzicato Rag* above is found in measures 66-67. Remember that the main symptom of Jethritis is an uncontrollable urge to swing on the eight-string.

*For a transcription of this solo, see *Mel Bay's Complete Jethro Burn's Mandolin Book*.

Jethritis

Dan Gelo

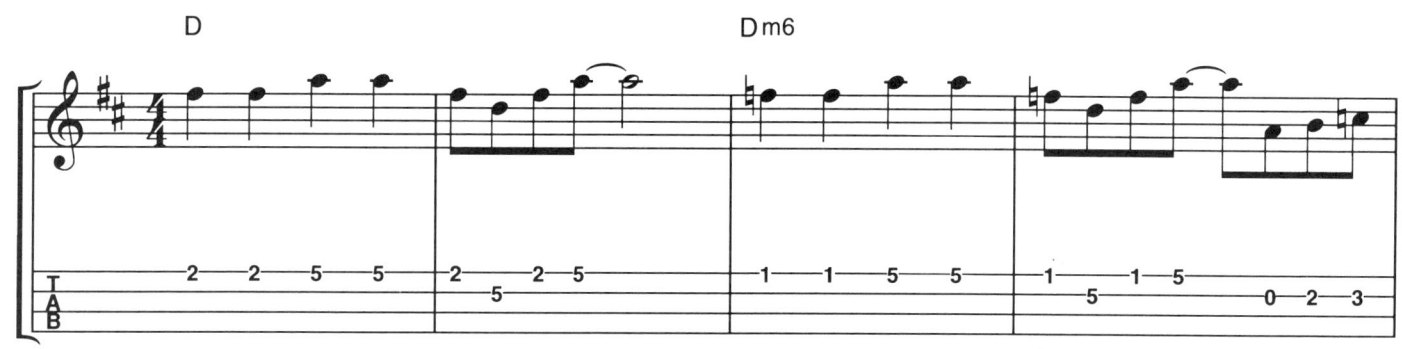
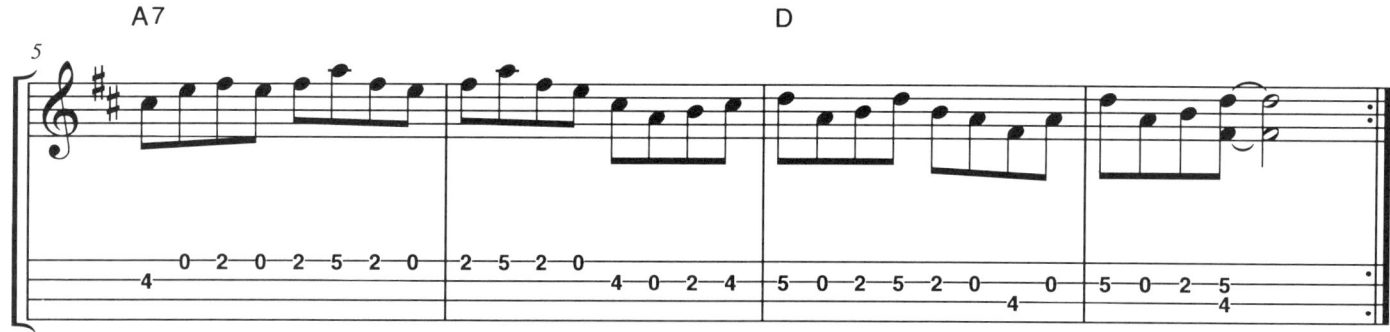
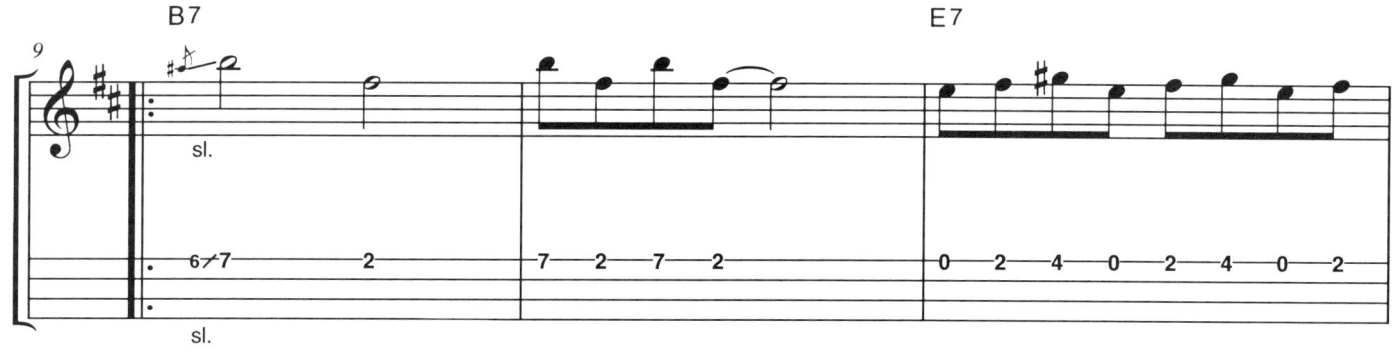
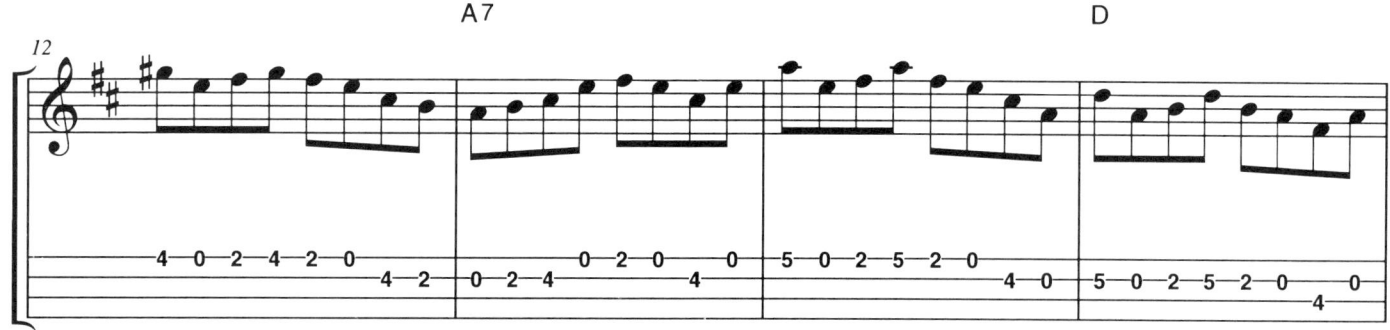

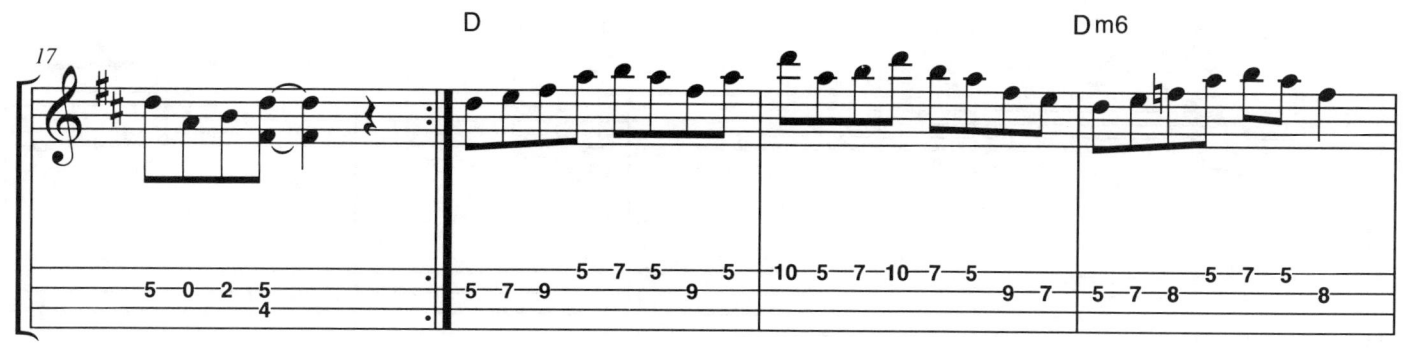
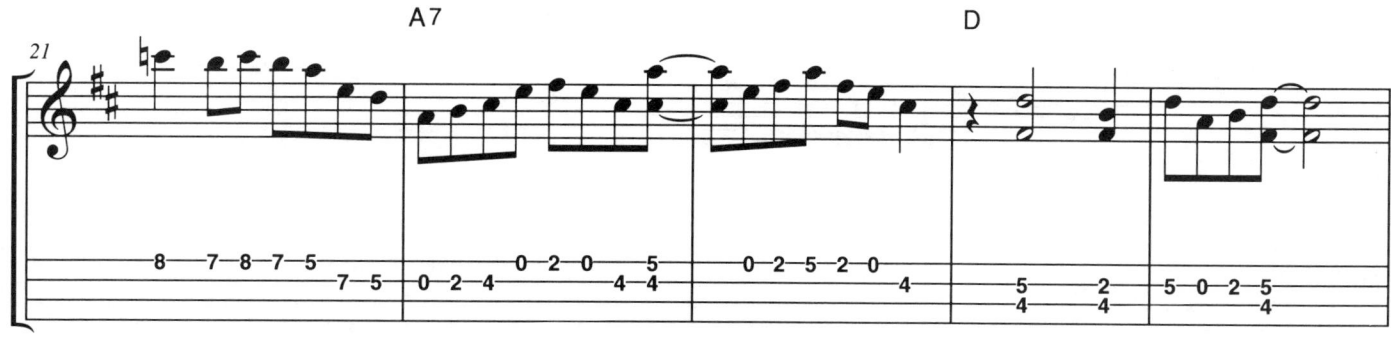
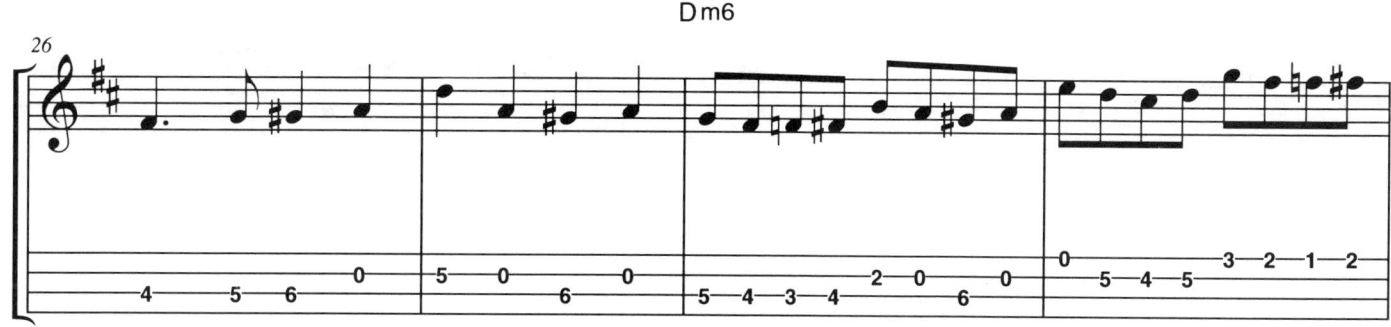
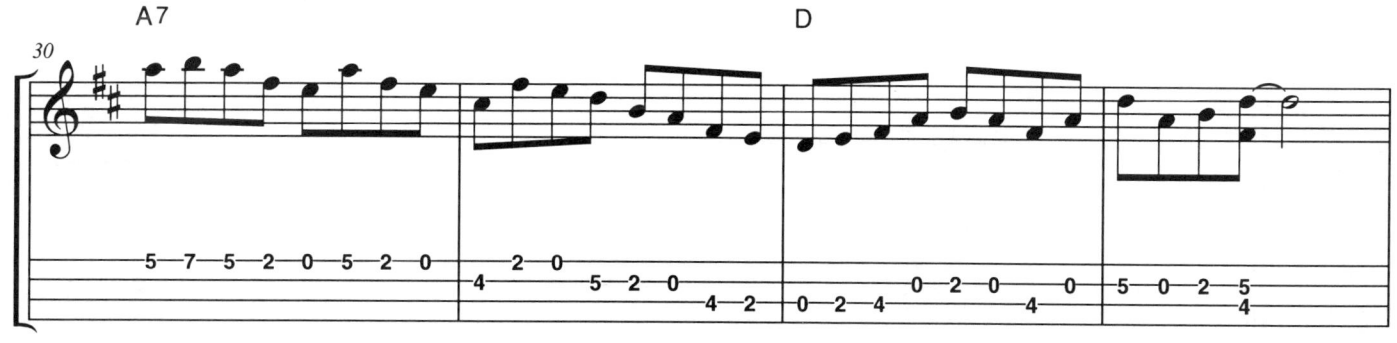

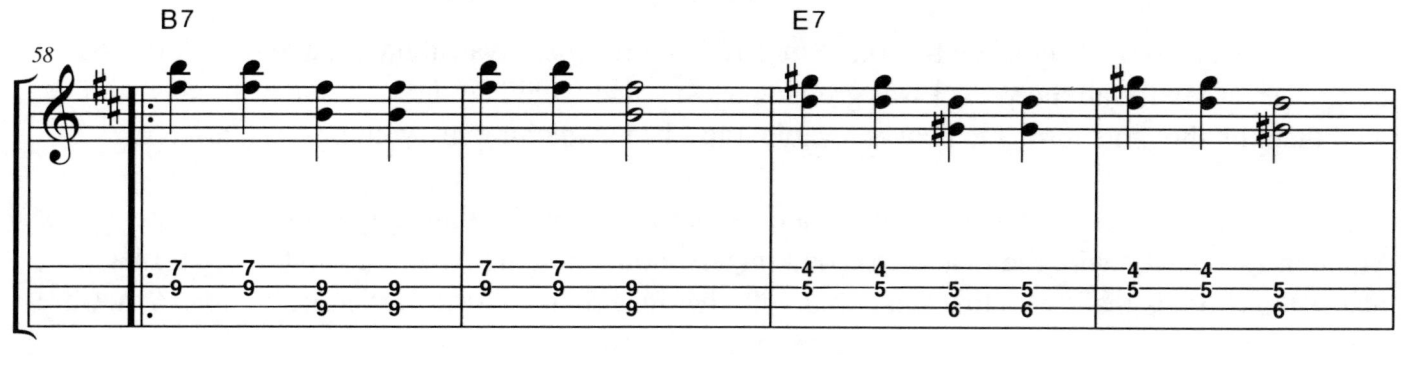
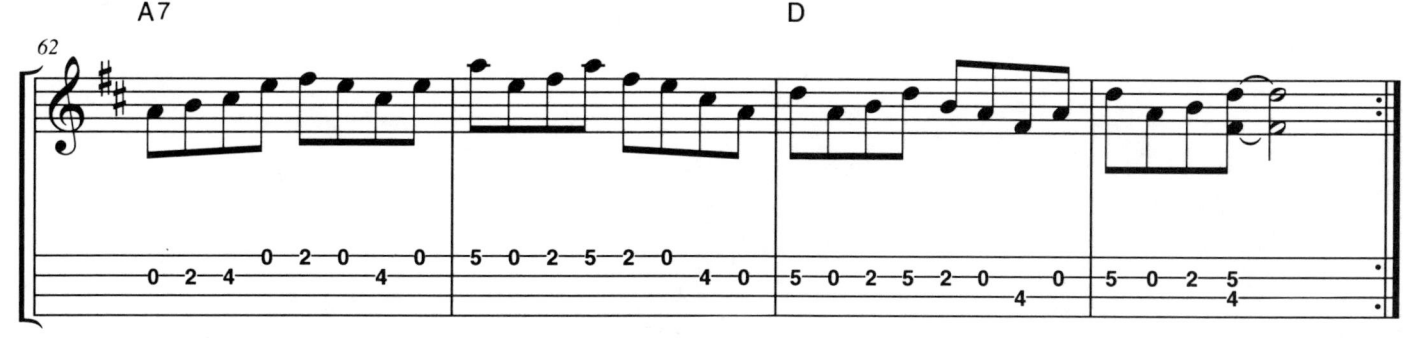
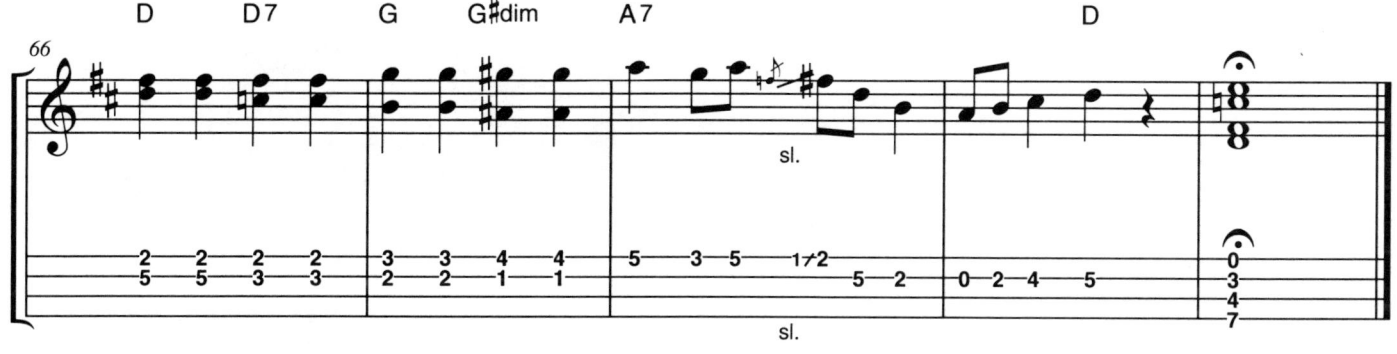

Father's Day

It was indeed Father's Day when this piece materialized for me. I was noodling and thinking about how, every week for all the years I was growing up, my dad would sit through music lessons with me. And then my thoughts turned to how enjoyable it has been watching my young sons learn too.

Father's Day is a chord solo that makes a lot of use of the open G string against various chord shapes. Much of it is played with the first and second fingers alone, moving up and down the neck. In a few places the chord is made of a first finger bar with the third finger added. Brush the chords so they are slightly arpeggiated and tremelo the top notes of the dotted half-note chords.

Father's Day

Dan Gelo

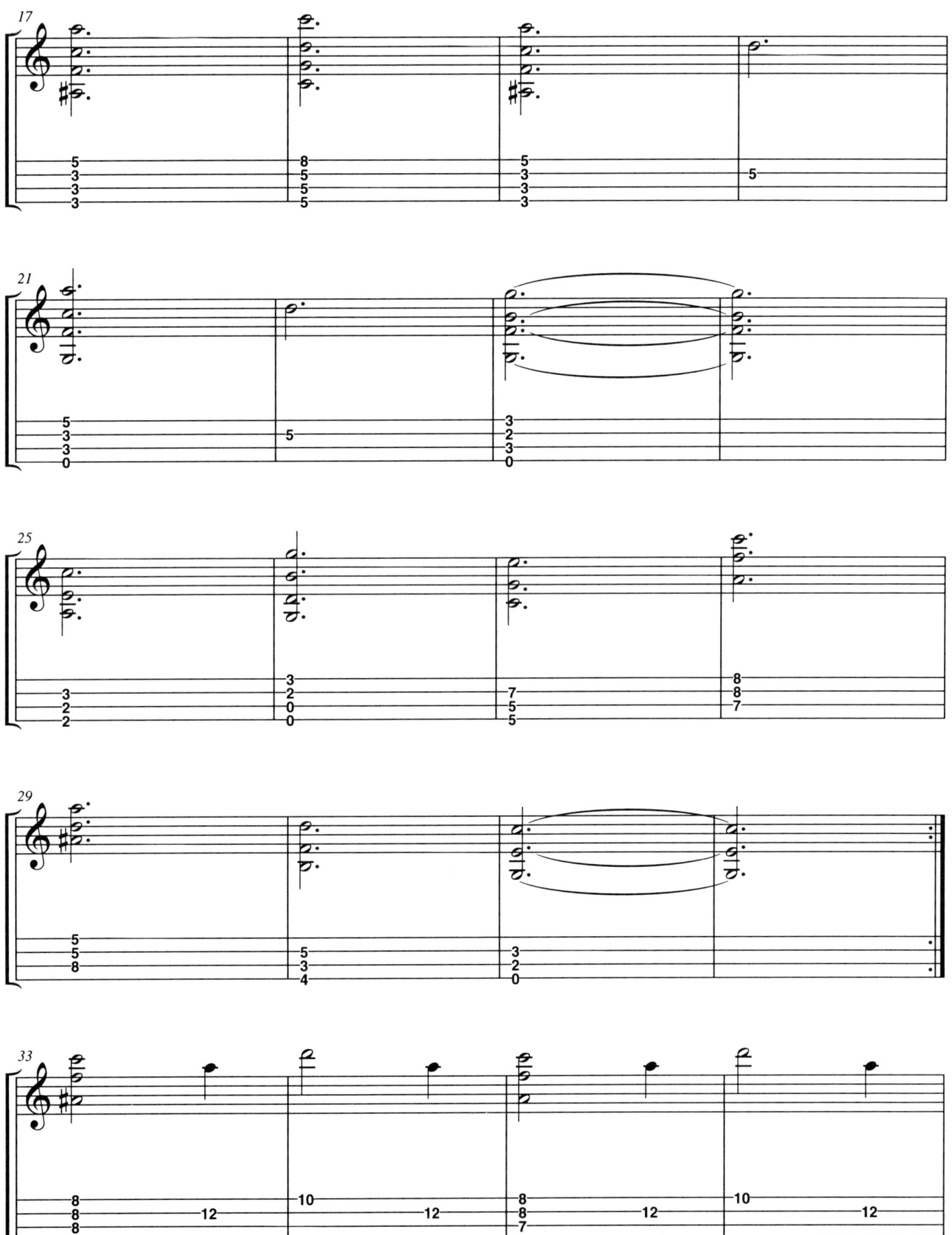

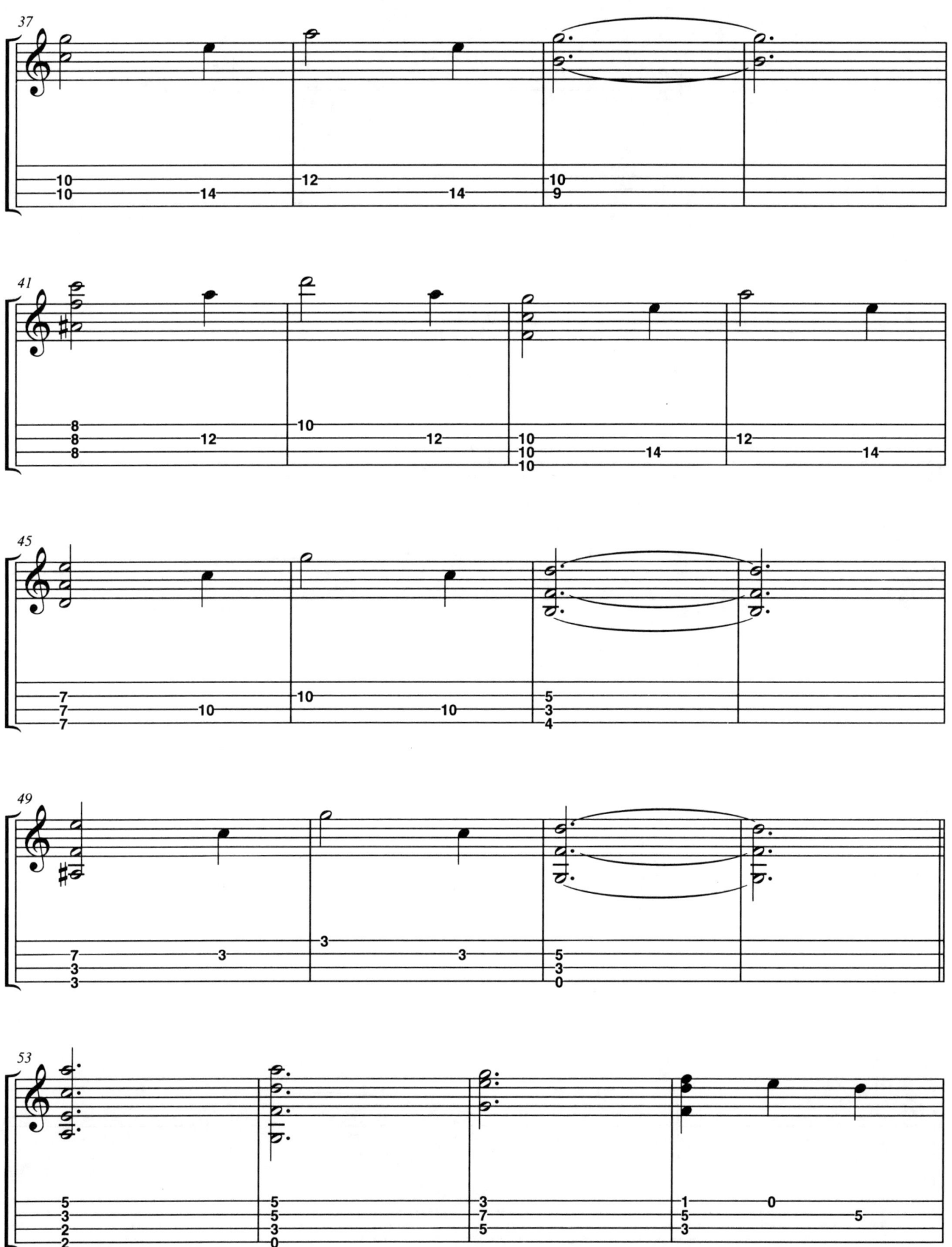

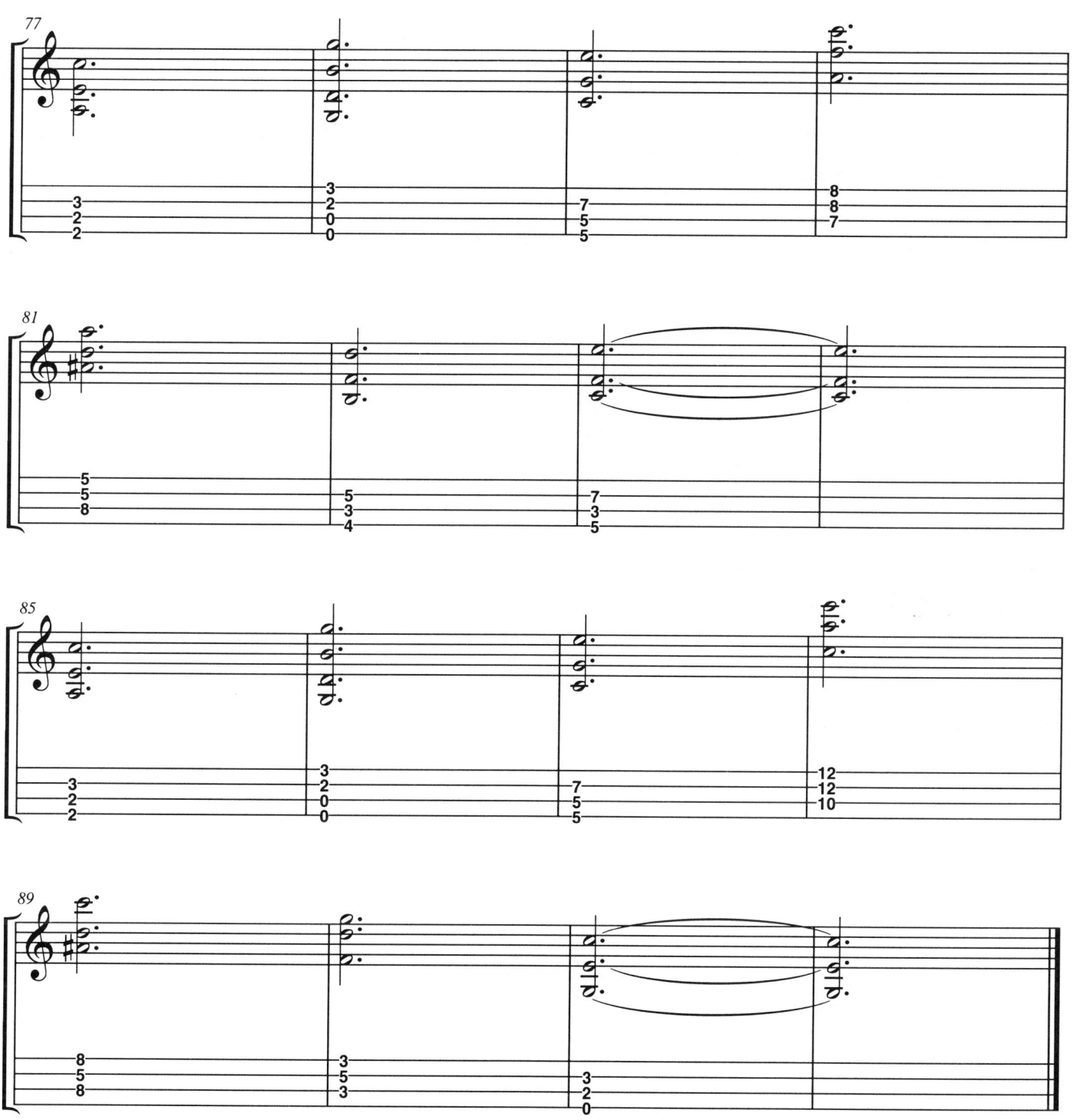